True Rebellion

VOLUME 1
Freedom from the Mind

Freedom from the Mind

Copyright © 2025 by Vishrant. All rights reserved.

No part of this book may be reproduced, stored in a retrieval system, or transmitted in any form or by any means, including electronic, mechanical, photocopying, recording, or otherwise, or translated into any language, without prior written permission from the author and publisher, except for brief quotations used in reviews or articles.

True Rebellion Vol. 1
Freedom from the Mind
ISBN:
978-1-7638511-2-2 - ebook
978-1-7638511-3-9 - paperback
The Vishrant Buddhist Society

Disclaimer

This book is intended for educational and informational purposes only. The insights and teachings shared within Freedom from the Mind reflect the personal experiences and understandings of Vishrant and are not intended as professional advice. The content of this book should not be used as a substitute for medical, psychological, legal, or financial advice. Readers are encouraged to use their discernment and seek professional guidance where necessary.

The author and publisher make no representations or warranties regarding the completeness, accuracy, or applicability of the teachings presented. The journey of self-inquiry and spiritual awakening is deeply personal, and each individual is responsible for their own path and experiences.

Contents

Overview 5
Introduction 7

CHAPTER ONE
True Rebellion 9

CHAPTER TWO
Doubt 25

CHAPTER THREE
The Razor's Edge of Enlightenment 39

CHAPTER FOUR
Love and Gratitude 63

CHAPTER FIVE
Celebrating Life 83

CHAPTER SIX
Seva 93

CHAPTER SEVEN
What Is Your Core Message? 107

CHAPTER EIGHT
Suffering and Addictions 131

CHAPTER NINE
Accessing Superconsciousness 143

CHAPTER TEN
Why Is Enlightenment An Inward Adventure? 167

CHAPTER ELEVEN
Why Higher Consciousness Is So Hard 193

CHAPTER TWELVE
Why Saying Yes Works 219

CHAPTER THIRTEEN
You Have Always Been At Your Final Destination 241

About Vishrant 265

Overview

True Rebellion is a four-part series delving deeply into the most crucial challenges faced by today's seekers. Vishrant's teachings are focused on seekers living and working in the marketplace, just as he did in his years-long journey towards Enlightenment.

Each volume of the True Rebellion series provides critical insight into the private workings of Vishrant's Mystic Heart Mystery School located in the hills of Perth near the historic Araluen Estate. Seekers from around the world attend in person and online in what may be the only Mystery School personally run by an enlightened master. Vishrant credits his years in Osho's Mystery School in Oregon and Pune for his own preparation for Enlightenment.

Vishrant sees that teachers who claim "there is nothing to do" are selling seekers short. He says seekers deserve the truth full strength and to understand that the obstacles that are in the way of Enlightenment must be undone if the seeker is to reach the ultimate. Although those who seek awakening must ultimately surrender themselves in the achievement, Vishrant's teachings are focused on helping ardent students of higher consciousness ready themselves for that awakening to occur.

The True Rebellion series was produced with this expressed purpose in mind: to highlight and deeply examine the key challenges and obstacles seekers face as hindrances to Enlightenment. The four-book series explores topics including family and work commitments, self-doubt, failure patterns, inherited programming, and the role of the mind and the need for scepticism, openness, present-moment awareness and trust on the path to higher consciousness and Enlightenment.

Vishrant's dialogues with students also provide numerous real-world examples from the master's own journey towards Enlightenment after he found himself as Truth in 1999 following many years of totality as a seeker. The exchanges recorded in the True Rebellion series contain Vishrant's trademark wit and humour, as well as the cutting insights and ruthless honesty he says every seeker must also develop for themselves.

Introduction

In the West we believe that we are the mind and the body, and we're firmly caught in that belief system that we are the mind and the body. And I know myself as Beingness or pure awareness. Everybody is pure awareness, but most people think they are a mind and a body that's been somewhere and is going somewhere. I know myself as pure awareness.

Everybody has that awareness. Everybody is that. But very few people are aware of it because it's not in our culture to even look for it – and everybody's aware of their mind. What's this that is aware? What's aware of the mind? What's aware of the thoughts? What's this that is aware? This is something we don't look at in the West at all, because when we do look at it, it doesn't move and it doesn't make noise, so it's not attractive. And we keep our awareness on that which makes noise and moves – typically the mind. And so what we truly are is actually missed.

Beingness is a word to describe something that can't be described. That which is aware of the mind can't be measured. It doesn't have boundaries. It's infinite. And it's silent and it's still. So trying to describe something which doesn't have any reference points is almost impossible. The only way that a person can understand it is for awareness itself to become aware of itself. And then they'll understand it, but they won't be able to explain it either. So I know what it is, but I can't tell you what it is. You have to find out for yourself.

So for someone in the West to "wake up" is very rare, because it's not our culture. If I hadn't been involved with Indian teachers, I wouldn't have had a clue as to Enlightenment or what Enlightenment really meant. I would've been pretty much the same as everyone else in Australia – interested in making money, building houses or getting a house, getting a relationship, having children – but I found there was something greater than me as an "I"; something greater that we all are: pure Being-ness.

CHAPTER ONE

True Rebellion

V: *dialog from Vishrant*
S: *dialog from student*
~ *separate dialogues from different speakers*

V: A lot of people feel that rebellion is something that you do against something that's happening outside of you, because you want to move into change outside of you. But the true rebellion has nothing to do with what's happening outside of you. It has everything to do with how you've been programmed as a human being because none of us were programmed for freedom. None of us were programmed for happiness. You think we would be, but we're not.

In fact, our default patterning of the ego is to constantly desire things to be different than how they are and this is not happiness, this is dissatisfaction. We have been fed so many belief systems that are limiting, and quite often not even real and when those belief systems and expectations aren't met, we go into contraction and take ourselves into lower consciousness.

So, the true rebellion is not against what's happening outside of you. It's about what's happening in your own mind. It's about examining the mind and developing an observer of the mind so you can see what the mind is up to, and then approaching every belief system that you have inside of yourself with doubt because when there is doubt in a belief system, we'll start to have a look at it, we'll start to examine it, we'll start to ask "Is this real or is it not real?"

The seeker moves into rebellion not outwardly, but inwardly against their programming, or in another way of saying it, against the brainwashing that has been done in their heads. After all, when you really examine your mind, you discover that you didn't program you. Genetics did, causality did, your parents, your schooling, your religion, your government, your peers – but you didn't program you.

In that programming process, you are fed a lot of belief systems that may or may not be true. For the seeker, they need to be examined because anything that brings about contraction in you as a result of an expectation not being met takes you into lower consciousness and takes you into sufferance.

Undoing the mind is essential, and it really occurs as a result of observing the mind first. That is where the rebellion begins. Watching the mind, just watching the mind, seeing what it does, seeing what it's up to and then starting to take the different belief systems that aren't true apart. And it's easy. All you've got to do is put doubt into any belief system, and it starts losing its power. It's going to be up to you. No one can do this for you. Someone might be able to help you by pointing out a few things for you, pointing out a few belief systems that you could examine, but really the work or the rebellion is in your court. You're the one who has to rebel.

All seekers are rebels. When we start looking, when we start observing our mind, the true rebellion has begun.

~

S: I have lived most of my life trying to be normal and fit in with society, but I've mostly struggled with that. Do I need to stop caring what people think of me in order to wake up?

V: Trying to be normal? I haven't. I'm not sure what normal is yet. If you want to wake up, all you have to do is learn unconditional surrender – and it's the hardest thing in the world to learn from the perspective of the mind because we are not in any way genetically programmed for it or causally programmed for it. We're programmed for survival, which means programmed to control, constantly. Unconditional surrender is foreign to us yet it is the doorway to super consciousness.

Can you surrender? Can you accept life as it is? That is the way that we learn surrender: through the practice of acceptance and letting go. Or are you going to resist, which is normal? All you need to learn if you're interested in waking up is unconditional surrender. We get there through practice, so you look at what you practise. Do you practise acceptance? Do you practise let go or do you practise resistance? Do you practise righteousness? Do you practise arrogance? What do you practise? Those who practise acceptance and let go eventually can surrender unconditionally. It doesn't happen because you think it's a good idea. It happens because of practice. What do you practise? People don't like that answer very much because it's very hard to do. It's very hard to surrender unconditionally. It's a death. And it's true, we have to die before we can know ourselves as Truth really. That's true too.

To surrender unconditionally is a death. When the Buddha sat under the Bodhi tree, he didn't sit under the Bodhi tree and meditate, he didn't sit under the Bodhi tree and self-inquire. He sat under the Bodhi tree and surrendered unconditionally – which is actually a non-doing – and awakening occurred. This is the way. Unconditional surrender is the way. And it is the mind that surrenders unconditionally. But that takes practice and that's all you need to know, nothing else.

~

S: What dies in unconditional surrender?
V: The dream that believes it's you, the "I". And with the "I" dies the survival mechanism, the primary survival mechanism of the body. After awakening, knowing self as Truth – or awareness aware of itself – there is no fear. Fear is completely gone. In Sanskrit it's called abhaya, fearlessness, because there's no fear anymore, it's gone. The primary survival mechanism has dropped. It's dropped with the "I" and instead of experiencing yourself as an imagined somebody, there's just nobody here. There's an absence. You're just here, but there's nobody here. There's pure Beingness, but nobody here.

That's freedom. It's absolute freedom. So awakening to our own true nature is just the best. The thing that dies is the one that's looking for awakening, the "I", the dream that believes it's had a past, that believes it has a future. Take away your imagination and it does not exist because it's not real. Who you truly are does. It's always here, pure Beingness.

~

S: How can you accept brutal rape unconditionally?
V: It may sound very callous of me to say that you can, but I've got to tell you that you can. In my own personal experience in this life, as a man, and as a teenager, I've had extremely nasty things occur in my life and I've found that I can accept them. The reason that I can accept them is because not to accept them creates suffering in me and I'm not willing to do that. No matter what has happened in this lifetime, I accept, because to turn myself in any way, shape or form into a victim would just be a continuance of what happened in the first place except this time instead of a perpetrator hurting me, I'm hurting me. I'm the one buying the victim story. I'm the one that is hurting me over and over again by seeing myself as a victim and I'm just not prepared to do that. It's bad enough things happen that are negative in the first place without you continuing it. It's up to you. If you can find acceptance for what it is, if you can actually find a way not to be a victim, you can be free. If you cannot, you will remain a prisoner of it, and that is your doing because you're creating it with your mind.

How free do you want to be? As long as you hang on to anything, you are a prisoner of whatever you're hanging on to and that's your doing, not someone else's doing. You are responsible. Negative things happen to us in this world, to every human being. We're the ones that can continue it, or stop it because we're in charge of our minds, your choice.

~

S: What will the practice of surrender look like when things are going wrong for me?

V: It won't look like anything because surrender doesn't have a look, it's a non-doing. So, things go wrong and there's just no reaction. For instance, if I was in physical pain, you wouldn't know because I wouldn't be reacting to it. Surrender is a non-doing. This is what the ego doesn't get. It doesn't get non-doing. It says, "How can I not do? How can I do surrender?" The ego can't. It's an absence. It's an absence of reaction. It's an absence, and it can only be achieved through practice. The practice of acceptance, the practice of letting go.

~

S: Since I started on a spiritual path, I have become less disturbed by negative events and circumstances of my life, but my family now think that I don't care, because I'm more detached. Can you please speak about the difference between being detached and not caring?

V: In my life I'm very detached from everything, but I care deeply about human beings, about animals, and I spend my life in service to try to help people because I care. But I am very detached, and being detached doesn't necessarily make you not care. When Heart opens, when Heart awakens, it affects the mind in such a way that it cares about everything and tries to take care of everything. This is the beauty of the Heart. This is how it affects the mind. It is lovely. From this detached space, there is just a life of service in the benefit of others, and this is beautiful.

This is the Way of the Heart. It's up to you. If you're willing to be open, you can find Heart. If you're not willing to be open, it's going to be difficult, because all of your defence systems, all of your closures are in the way of you perceiving love. It's up to you. Every time we close, because we get angry at something, we cut ourselves off from our own Heart. And we bring more darkness and more violence into the world. If we stay open, and we start perceiving love, we can become an oasis of that. And we can bring more of that into the world. But we are responsible for how our mind is. Nobody else is doing it to us. We create our thoughts. We create the way we are in the world. We are 100 per cent responsible. We can't blame others for how we are not in reality, because we're responsible. You create your reality by the way you think.

~

S: I've heard it said that it is the nature of man for the Heart to open and close like a flower. Is this true?
V: I really wouldn't know. Open and close like a flower. That's very poetic. Look, if you stay open, love is there and you perceive it. If you keep closing, of course you're cutting yourself off from it. That's a given. But you're responsible for the closure, so you're responsible for the cutting off. If you remain open, Heart and love is always here, because it's always here. It's only not here when you're closed

or somehow defended. Find out for yourself. Practice openness. When you start practising openness, you're going to discover how closed you are, how defended you are. And that gives you an opportunity to either take down those defences and open up or remain closed. It's up to you. You create your reality. Nobody else does.

Higher consciousness is achieved through openness not through closure. It's achieved through being undefended, not defended. You won't find someone with higher consciousness who is closed. If they are, they've gone back down to lower consciousness. One thing everybody who I've ever met who's awake has in common is they're wide open, undefended, vulnerable. That's got to tell you something. There was a price that was paid for that. That doesn't happen by itself, because it's against nature. Higher consciousness is against nature. So is Enlightenment. Because in nature, we defend ourselves, we protect ourselves, we survive.

Only human beings can go beyond that because they can learn to surrender, they can learn to accept, they can learn to let go. It's up to you. You're creating your reality. Nobody's creating it for you. It's up to you.

~

S: Sometimes people in group situations will draw others into their negativity. What can I do to stop myself from being drawn in by the negativity of others?
V: It's a choice, isn't it? You can listen to someone's negativity and not buy it or you can buy it. Your choice. The question would indicate that you think

you have no choice. Of course you have a choice. You don't have to buy people's negativity. You can stay detached from it. It's up to you. Why would you want to buy it anyway? It just takes you down the chute. It's already taken them down the chute. Why do you want to go with them?

~

S: I see you as a rebel. Did you become a rebel because you wanted to change the world?

V: Heck no! I became a rebel because I didn't like school teachers. I didn't like bullies. I didn't like my parents. I didn't like the life I had as a child. I rebelled against it. I was what was considered an uncontrollable child. And so I did rebel. And I got into a lot of trouble. In my era, the consequence for rebellion was a beating and I was beaten every day at school because I did not comply. I was a rebel back then. But it wasn't until I got to about 18 or 19 that I realised the true rebellion is not outside of you. It's inside of you. It's how you've been brainwashed. It's how you've been programmed. You've been programmed to be a prisoner. The true rebellion is inside of you.

~

S: There is a saying by Gandhi, "Be the change that you want to see in the world." What is your opinion on this statement?

V: Yeah. Okay. People get into this rebellion idea. And they go out and they protest and they go out with anger. Well, what they're doing is taking more violence into the world. And violence doesn't fix things. It makes things worse. But people think somehow their violent nature is somehow going to do some good and violence doesn't do good. Violence is bad. You want to change the world? Change yourself. "Be the change," as Gandhi has put. Become a loving, kind, generous person. Become someone who takes care of others, someone who picks up the rubbish that other people drop on the road, someone who can make a difference because they have changed inside of themselves. If all you do is go out there and shake your fist in anger, you're not moving to change. You're just bringing more violence into the world. You're bringing more darkness into the world. You're not lighting anything.

Do you really want to make a change? Change inside yourself. You become the change. There's a thing in the Hindu religion called ahimsa, which means non-violence. Ahimsa is a way of life. But it's not just non-violence outside of you. It's also non-violence inside of yourself. Anger is violence. Have a look and see. When we project it at someone else, we're being violent towards them, and when we're just angry, we're being violent to ourselves. Have a look and see. Be the change inside of you. Be that change that you want to see in the world. You be the change. Gandhi got it right.

~

S: What is the most effective way to see the parts of my psyche that I'm unaware of?
V: Well, developing that silent witness is the only way really. I don't know if there is another way. Get involved with a group of people who are willing to tell

you the truth about you – not a group of people who just want to tell you how wonderful you are because they want your acceptance. But get involved with a group of people who are willing to tell you what they can see about you. Those people will help you see more about what's happening inside of you. That is an effective way, to have friends who are willing to tell you what is going on in you.

From my perspective, I've always enjoyed the people who have been willing or have the courage to tell me what they can see about me, even if it's negative, because sometimes in the past I wasn't able to see. So besides developing a silent witness that watches the mind, having a group of friends who are willing to tell you the truth about what they can see about you is brilliant, particularly if those friends have some acumen, particularly if they have higher consciousness themselves, because they're going to see things that are really valuable for you to see. Who you associate with is going to affect you a great deal. If all you do is hang out with people who tell you how lovely you are, you're not going to see much. How about hanging out with the ones who tell you how bad you are? They're probably going to be your better teachers.

~

S: Without being identified with it, the "I" appears to be an entity comprised of body and conditioned mind. How to remove this identification?

V: From the perspective of the mind, it's not actually possible. The only way that the identification can drop is if you know yourself as Truth. When awareness is aware of itself, it is absolutely impossible for the mind to think that it is a somebody because it is seen for what it is: a dream that is not real that is based in projections and memories, neither being real. But that is because awareness is aware of itself. The only true way to become unidentified, for the "I" to drop, is to wake up to your true nature and stay awake. That's called Enlightenment. That's the only possibility. The "I" trying to be unidentified from itself is just the "I" playing games with itself. Every now and again I've had people trying to talk without using the word "I". It sounds so ridiculous. You want to be unidentified? Wake up.

~

S: I find that when I can tune into the energy of Beingness, I lose touch with the world out here. How do you interact with others while still keeping your awareness on Beingness?

V: That's an old question. In the early stages of awareness finding itself, it's very hard because you've got awareness on awareness and you haven't got much awareness out here. One of my early teachers used to say that what can happen is you can have one foot in and one foot out. In other words, awareness on awareness, and awareness also out through the mind in the world. But that takes a bit of practice because quite often when awareness goes out into the world, it leaves itself, so there is a sense of losing Beingness, losing that expanded reality that you found.

From my perspective, that flip flopping occurred for more than 12 months where I'd find myself as

Beingness, then I'd find myself as ego, then I'd find myself as Beingness. It was in the unconditional surrendering of the mind, in an ongoing way, that allowed awareness to start to really lock onto itself. So, awareness didn't shift. It got so locked on, it didn't shift. Then being in the world and negotiating the world became possible from having awareness on awareness. It didn't shift, but I'm not going to say that was that easy either. It's difficult. I used to practise in Satsang with my teachers, because when I was with my teachers, I'd find awareness would sit on itself. I'd practise talking to them, which means awareness was also out as well as being in. So there was a practice of having awareness out, while awareness was locked onto itself, in Satsang, with my teachers, and that became continuous about 21 years ago. It's like awareness, like two magnets came together, and they locked on. Awareness locked onto itself. But there was a year of what I would call flip flopping, which I believe John de Ruiter called "half-baked Enlightenment", where you can find Beingness, but you lose it, you go back to the "I". It's not full Enlightenment. It is half-baked Enlightenment. Practice is what works. Find someone who's awake and practise with them.

~

S: You mentioned that you initially rebelled because you didn't like your teachers and parents. How did you find your motivators and drivers in life and then change them?

V: I think we need to go a little deeper into the story of why the original rebellion began. As a child,

I had ADHD and dyslexia and it was undiagnosed so I couldn't get acceptance. I was all over the place because my concentration was very limited and everyone tried to bring me into line through discipline rather than understanding that I actually had a couple of conditions that weren't that helpful. So instead of complying, I just rebelled. I went wild really. I stopped looking for acceptance completely from outside of myself and did whatever I wanted to do. This is a true rebellion, but it's an uncomfortable rebellion.

The true rebellion, the real rebellion is really when you get inside your own mind and you get to have a look at how you've been programmed. Then you discover your motivators. I'd had a relatively hard time at school, and a relatively hard time at home, so one of my main motivators was anger, and it is such a destructive motivator because it has no Heart in it and it's ruthless. But that was one of my motivators when I was very young. It was a motivator that I got to examine when I was 19, because I could see the damage it was doing and I saw the pattern of how anger worked, how I would actually get touched. Something would hurt and then anger – which is fuelled by blame – would come out, and that took me away from the hurt and empowered me. So I was avoiding my own pain and those touches through anger. It was my defence system.

But what a destructive thing to do, because it doesn't build bridges, it destroys them. I started to really watch the anger and I'd watch the touch, and instead of going to anger, I'd allay it. In other words, my mind stopped supporting the reaction of anger. It stopped supporting the defence system of anger. Instead, it allowed me to feel what was touched instead of defending it. That was a brilliant thing to do because anger is just not good. It hurts people. It destroys relationships. It might empower you, but at what cost?

We don't need to be empowered in that way. We can be powerful without being angry. All we've got to do is be willing to meet that touch. Allow ourselves to feel that touch without reacting with blame. This is the way to higher consciousness. This is the path of true rebellion.

Thank you for Satsang. Good to see you bravehearts here today.

CHAPTER TWO

Doubt

V: Doubt is the healthiest thing a human being can actually have because all of us have been brainwashed. We've been made to believe a great deal of things that aren't our own direct experience and we live our lives based on these beliefs. In a lot of ways, we live our lives falsely because the beliefs don't hold water. The seeker is like a scientist and approaches everything with a little doubt, to check it out to make sure it's true. Prove it to me.

One of the first things that I got involved with after I left school was examining the belief systems that had been given to me by my society, my religion, my parents and my peers because I could see clearly that there were a lot of holes in them, even though everybody I knew believed the same thing, particularly as a Catholic. There was something not right there. It was all based on belief. It wasn't based on any form of reality. There was no evidence, in other words, so I had to start questioning everything because I could see that these different beliefs that I had were keeping me imprisoned in some way.

I had a strong belief at the age of 19 in victim-orientated thinking: that other people could make me feel, that other people were responsible for my feelings. This belief system alone creates so much suffering in human beings because they turn themselves into victims of existence, of other people, of life in general, and suffer incredibly. And you don't have to ever, ever be a victim. Look, bad things may happen. Things go down that you don't agree with, but you don't have to be a victim of them. You can volunteer to be a victim of it because you believe you are a victim, but are you really? Isn't that just a belief? Life is just the way it is. Things happen. Good and bad things happen. We don't have to hold the belief that we're a victim of anything – and if we remove that one belief, our whole life changes because the belief in being a victim or being able to be a victim creates so much suffering in us and we don't need to do that.

The second belief that I challenged aggressively was the belief in worry; thinking somehow that worry was going to sort out my problems – that somehow, magically, worry was going to make things better for me if I toss things around in my head, long enough, thinking about them. So I stopped that one too. Because heck, I looked at my own family, and saw well, what's worry ever done for any of the members of my family, or anybody I know? I love what Francis of Assisi said about it. He said it cannot make a man an inch taller. Well, it can't. As a matter of fact, it can't do anything except make you feel bad. So the first two beliefs I removed from my system were a belief in victim-orientated thinking, the belief that I could be a victim of anything, and the belief in worry.

And gosh, what a wonderful thing to do for yourself, to remove those two beliefs that create suffering for your whole life. And of course, that came about as a result of doubt. I started to doubt that I was a victim. I started to doubt that worry actually worked and was worthwhile keeping. Doubt is something the seeker uses to examine what may or may not be real, and eventually it'll take them home. You remove everything, you take everything away that creates contraction in you, any belief system you have that creates contraction, and you put doubt into it. The moment you put doubt into any belief system it loses its power.

I think I was about 33 when I got to see I was still full of belief systems. I sat down one night and I just started writing them out. And I was writing until four or five in the morning, the different tiny belief systems that I had, that I never truly examined. They were just taken for granted because everybody I knew believed the same thing. I wrote them on little bits of paper and I threw them in the fire because I had a fireplace. That wasn't enough. I wish it was.

The only way you can truly undo belief systems is by putting doubt into them. I'm not the sort of person who has faith in anything. I trust what's real. I trust what I know to be real. With that, the mind can be quite clean. It doesn't get caught in contracting because of all these false beliefs we have about how we think life should run. From my perspective, to have doubt is to have a healthy mind. It's not a sheep-like mind, it's a mind that will examine. It's a mind that will help set you free. But that's up to you. You're going to create your reality with the way you think. Have a look at all of the belief systems inside you and see if any of them hold water. Just because the whole society might believe something does not make it true.

Any questions, any statements, any challenges to this teaching today?

S: Is there anything that you don't doubt?

V: Yeah, there's one thing. My mind does not doubt that I am Beingness, that I am that, because that is so, and it's the only thing that my mind actually trusts, the silence and stillness of Beingness. That can always be trusted.

S: Did you have that trust before awakening?

V: To some degree, yes, because I'd been a meditator for a lot of years. Twenty-odd years before awakening. And I loved the silence, I loved the stillness, I loved no-mind. I loved that peace that comes with that. I also got to see that my mind was a bullduster that actually told itself lies and then justified those lies, so I recognised clearly that even my mind wasn't to be trusted. There needed to be doubt there to question everything. After all, we didn't program ourselves. Our parents programmed us. Our schooling programmed us. Our peers programmed us. Our religion programmed us. Our country programmed us. It's not a bad idea to get a bit suspicious of it all and have a look. Were they right? Were their belief systems correct? And with all their belief systems, did it make them happy? Did it set them free?

~

S: Will you please talk about the relationship between doubt and acceptance?

V: Okay, so my mind pretty much doubts everything, but accepts everything at the same time. The reason for that is very simple. My mind understands the key to freedom. The key to freedom is acceptance. One of the ways that we can't accept is because we have strong beliefs that aren't true. A part of moving to acceptance is to understand how the mind ticks and then putting doubt into some of the beliefs so they don't contract us anymore. So there's definitely a connection.

We witness the mind just by watching it. Then we get to see how many lies it tells us if we approach it with doubt, which is a scientific approach. If we approach it with faith, we're going to have filters that protect it so we're not going to see clearly. When we approach something with doubt, we see things way more clearly because we don't have a filter there of wanting it to be so.

~

S: Where does attitude come from? Don't our thoughts determine our attitude?
V: Yes, of course they do.
S: So why give up positive thinking if it can improve my attitude, and help me be more successful?
V: I've never suggested giving up positive thinking, I've just suggested don't entertain negative thinking. I also don't teach positive thinking because it's just another thing that you have to somehow let go of. Just let go of negative thinking and you're naturally buoyant. All humans are naturally buoyant. The only thing that sinks them is negative thinking. I've never suggested giving up positive thinking. I just don't

promote it as a way. I don't promote positive affirmations. It's just another way the mind gets engaged.

I'm not interested in engaging the mind. I'm interested in going beyond the mind. What sinks people – what keeps people in lower consciousness – is negative thinking. Just remove all of that. That's best. Don't get involved in negative thinking. You've got to remember from what I was saying before, victim-orientated thinking is also negative thinking. It'll take you down every time.

~

S: Is it a good idea to doubt even what a spiritual teacher tells you?
V: Heck yeah, especially what spiritual teachers tell you. Check it out for yourself. I never, ever ask anyone to believe me. Oh please don't. Find out what I'm saying for yourself, check it out for yourself. Make it your knowing. Anyone who just collects belief systems from teachers is going to get lost. I'm just pointing in a certain direction that you can look for yourself. Look there and find out for yourself. Always doubt your teachers. Always doubt your teachers and check it out for yourself.

~

S: You talk about only trusting our own direct experience. Why shouldn't we doubt this? Couldn't we have misinterpreted our own experience?
V: Well, that's a possibility. Keep looking. Keep watching. Keep witnessing the mind until it becomes clear for you. Don't give up. To become a witness of the mind is just brilliant because you get to see how much rubbish it holds. You get to see. You get to see

how deluded you've actually been. You get to see how you value things that don't truly have value because you've taken on society's value system. Keep looking, keep looking, be a scientist of your mind, investigate, lift all the rocks to see what's under them. Become curious. This is the seeker.

~

S: Do planetary positions affect our lives, or is this also belief?

V: The truth is I don't know. I suspect there might be something in it, but the bottom line is I don't really know and I'm quite happy with "I don't know". People want to know so they can somehow have control over their environment. The truth is, most of the time, we don't know, but we pretend to know because it makes us feel safe. When you're willing to sit in "I don't know" you become innocent again. You become fresh again. There's no innocence in knowing, there's no freshness in knowing. It's all stale because it's in the mind. The beginner's mind doesn't know and allows the universe to flow through. And this is beautiful. So to that question, I don't know.

~

S: Does to doubt my mind mean I don't trust my gut feeling?

V: You can trust your gut feeling and still doubt what you're actually feeling. Why not? Why not look? Why not become a scientist of your own mind? One of the things I enjoyed about studying Gautama the Buddha was that he was a scientist. He was a scientist of his own mind. He watched his own mind, he saw how it ticked, and as a result raised his consciousness levels to a degree where he could wake up. But you don't raise the consciousness levels of your mind by believing it. You raise the consciousness levels of your mind by watching it and taking it apart. Faith just keeps you ignorant.

~

S: Is blind faith and trust the same thing?

V: I've never considered them the same. Faith demands some kind of belief system. Trust doesn't necessarily demand any belief system. I love the bit about trusting in God, let go and trust God, I like that bit. That means you completely let go of control and you're not trusting because you have a belief that you're going to be taken care of. You don't know. You're just trusting – and with faith there is usually a belief system that somehow things are going to be okay. Well, I don't like faith one bit because I don't like belief systems, but I do love trust. Let go, trust God. It's brilliant.

S: Does faith have anything to do at all with gaining higher consciousness?

V: Not in my understanding, no. Faith is usually based on belief systems that I don't support. Why would I be interested in belief systems I don't support? If you study all of the old masters, you'll see they all say the same thing: surrender. That's it. You're looking for something to learn? Just practise surrender. You master surrender and you've mastered your mind. You've mastered your mind? Then your mind is prepared for Enlightenment. No faith required.

~

S: When I start doubting my own mind, I start to feel unsettled and confused. If I doubt everything, how can I know what is certain and real?

V: Yeah, this is the plight of the seeker. You get to a point when you start doubting, where you realise there's no purpose in life either except maybe life itself. All of the other purposes that have been fed to you in the form of belief systems are rubbish. Then you wonder, "Well, what am I going to do here? If there's no purpose to life, what am I going to do here?" Well, what came to me was pretty simple: serve Heart. Then your life is beautiful here. Those who choose to serve Heart, the noble path, have beautiful lives.

And yes, you do get unstable when you start challenging your mind. That's part of the deal. Freedom from the rubbish that's in your mind only occurs when you undo it, and when we undo anything, it can get messy. You can get pretty fragile. That's part of the deal – or would you rather just keep all the false belief systems? It's up to you. This is your game. This is your game of higher consciousness. No one else is going to play it for you. If you just believe everything that's been put into your mind, wow, you're going to stay pretty ignorant.

~

S: Is it possible to trust the mind at all?

V: We have to trust the mind to some degree, but what I'm really saying about not trusting is not to trust all of the belief systems that have been put into you since birth.

We have a belief system that people shouldn't betray us, and people get so contracted when other people betray them. Yet everybody betrays. To actually have a belief system that people shouldn't betray us is out of touch with the reality of the world we live in. Yet people still contract over it and get upset. People murder people over it. To remove just that one belief system relieves a great deal of suffering. I do not have a belief system that people shouldn't betray me, or lie to me, or cheat. I don't. I removed those belief systems because I just was not into my own suffering.

~

S: How do I know if I'm in tune with my inner knowing or just believing my mind?
V: You don't. The mind is so tricky. It will pretend to be inner knowing. The one thing that I know about inner knowing is it just knows, it doesn't use words, it doesn't try to convince you of anything. That's always the ego. It doesn't justify its position ever. It just knows which way to go. If this thing that's calling itself inner knowing is trying to convince you of anything, if it's using words, it is not inner knowing, it's the mind pretending to be inner knowing. Inner knowing just knows which way to go. It just knows.
S: Is that healthy, to have a balance of doubt and positivity?
V: Is it healthy? The healthiest thing a human being can do is wake up to their own true nature because as long as you're living as an ego, living as something that is false, you're actually living as a dream. It's

best to learn to die before the body does. Wake up to your own true nature. There is nothing healthier than knowing yourself as Truth.

~

S: Why would my mind lie to me? And who is this me that's lied to?

V: Yes, good question. You won't find the "me" anywhere. It's imagined. The "I" is imagined. It doesn't exist in reality. Without imagination, the "I" or the "me" – whatever you want to call it – doesn't exist. It seems to exist, but only because people hold it in their memory and their projections. The truth is the "I" doesn't exist. It is not there. And when you move firmly into the moment, there is no sense of "I". The "I" exists out of time. It is the past. You have a look. Try finding the "I" anywhere. You won't find it. It just doesn't exist. Yet it seems to exist. What's of interest isn't the "I". What's aware of the mind? What's aware of this thing that claims to be "me"? What's this that is pure consciousness? Find that. That's of interest. The mind is not interesting. What the mind appears in, the background, that's interesting.

~

S: What's the difference between having healthy doubt and being completely untrusting?

V: I trust everything because I'm a fatalist. Doesn't mean I don't doubt it. I trust everything. I trust that everything's happening exactly as it's meant to be. There are no mistakes because whatever is happening is meant to be happening, otherwise it wouldn't be happening. I trust that. That doesn't mean I don't have doubts about different people and different things that are going on, but from a place of trust. I'm not in resistance to life. Life's the way it is.

People don't understand trust. You don't get anything from trust. Trust is a death. It's like unconditional surrender is the end, it's over. So be it. There is no business deal that you can offer Truth. The only deal if you want to wake up, the only deal is everything for Truth and nothing for you. Everything for God and nothing for you. Everything for Beingness and nothing for you. There is no other deal. If there's something in it for you, awakening won't occur. There's too much ego involved.

~

S: If you trust, how can you doubt?
V: Easy. We've got intelligent minds. We can trust completely that everything's meant to be the way it is, but we can still doubt people's intentions. We can still doubt what's actually happening because we're intelligent. We can see that there's something afoot. We can see there is something amiss and we can accept it. We don't have to go into resistance to it. We can trust that that's what's meant to be happening, even though we can see that it's not right, because we're intelligent.

I can see quite clearly when people are trying to lie to me or cheat me or somehow run me down. I can see it very clearly, but I trust that's meant to be happening otherwise it wouldn't be happening. Have a look and see.

~

S: Did you ever go through a period of doubting your commitment to higher consciousness?
V: Yes, I did. I fell out of love with the Rajneesh organization for a while because I had some disagreements over policy that they had regarding fundraising and I fell out of love with the religion.

I stayed away for six months, until a friend of mine committed suicide. I had a look at my life again and asked "Well, what am I doing?" I had just partied for six months. I had a look at it and said, "You know, we're so temporary here, we're all going to die, its best that I go for higher consciousness. It's best that I go for Enlightenment while I have a chance, while I have a living master."

So I got my sannyas back again, because I'd thrown my mala at one of the leading women in charge of the centre in Fremantle because I was so upset with the way they were behaving. I got it back and became a sannyasin again.

I did doubt. Definitely doubted. But the recognition of the impermanence of life, brought about by the suicide of my friend, pushed me right back into it. It's best to die before the body does. It's best to wake up here.

Thank you for Satsang. Good to see you bravehearts here today.

CHAPTER THREE

The Razor's Edge of Enlightenment

V: Welcome to satsang.
S: Hello Vishrant, can you please talk about what it means to walk on the razor's edge of Enlightenment?
V: As you go higher in consciousness, it is more difficult to stay. It is easy to fall as all we've got to do is contract, all we've got to do is resist and we fall. Someone who's really high in consciousness is not reacting, is not resisting, and is not defeating themselves with contraction.

In the earliest stages of raising consciousness levels, the path is quite wide. You can make a lot of mistakes. You can fail a great deal, but if you're going higher and higher and higher, to stay that high, you don't contract, you don't resist. You have a mind that is equanimous, a mind that stays even, even while under fire. Otherwise, well, you can't stay there. As soon as you contract, you fall. You go back to lower consciousness.

Now at a higher level again, particularly in the early days if someone wakes up, where awareness has become aware of itself, there's the potential for awareness to pull away from itself and go back to the mind, go back to ego-based reality, and that potential is relatively high. It occurs when someone goes into contraction, into resistance to life, and awareness goes back to the ego, to the mind, and seemingly – but not really – Beingness is lost. Beingness can't be lost. It's always here. It's just that it is no longer aware of itself.

So the razor's edge at the highest level, in the early days of Enlightenment, is to keep awareness on awareness. The mind stays peaceful, it doesn't contract, it doesn't resist. After a while it seems that becomes very stable, a little bit like two permanent magnets locking on and very hard to pull apart, no matter what is happening. For someone to wake up, they need a mind that will not go to war with the world, will actually stay calm, will stay relaxed, and will stay relatively peaceful. This type of mind will support higher consciousness and Enlightenment. This kind of mind doesn't support suffering because it's not contracting, it's not resisting.

As we go up in consciousness levels, all the obstacles that are in the way of higher consciousness and Enlightenment, basically anything that contracts us, the defence systems, any belief systems that cause resistance taking us into lower consciousness are removed so a person can stay at a higher level of consciousness and they can stay awake. In Buddhism, it's about developing a mind that is equanimous, a mind that stays level, and even no matter what is happening, even while under fire, it stays level. It doesn't contract. It doesn't go into resistance. It supports Truth. It supports Heart. This is relatively difficult because we grew up in a society where we contract, where we resist, where we turn ourselves into victims of this and that. Of course, that keeps people very much locked in lower consciousness and suffering. In higher consciousness, that's not a go. No resistance, no contraction. Acceptance of life as it is is the way. When bad things happen, or negative things happen, there's an acceptance of it rather than a resistance against it, and sometimes this is called the razor's edge. It's easy to fall off. It is such a narrow, narrow edge. It's easy to go back to contraction and to go back to ego-based reality.

People do self-inquiry and they find themselves as Truth and then they find themselves back as ego-based reality. It's because awareness has gone back to the mind, it's gone back to the ego – usually because the mind has contracted over something, has gone into resistance over something. For the spiritual aspirant to develop a mind that will support Enlightenment, there is a fair bit of work so contraction doesn't occur, resistance doesn't occur.

Of course, this is up to you. No one can do it for you. Someone who's awake can show you which way to go. They can talk to you about acceptance, they can talk to you about different types of resistance, different defence systems that are in the way, but they can't do the work for you. You have to do the work. And just seeing it, which is insight, is not enough. It does need to get undone. The mind needs to get undone so it doesn't constantly react and go into resistance to life. Acceptance is the key.

Are there any questions, any statements, any challenges to this teaching today?

S: Is there a skill or pattern that I can develop as a foundation that makes the process of higher consciousness easier?

V: Yes, a pattern of watching the mind. If you develop a pattern of witnessing the mind, you get to see what it's up to. If you don't have a pattern of witnessing the mind, you don't see what it's up to. So how can you stop it from anything? If you can't see what the mind is doing, how can you actually surrender it? How can you move to acceptance? How can you allay it?

It's essential that you be able to see what's happening. And this comes as a result of witnessing the mind. Being a witness to the mind, instead of being judgmental, instead of analysing, instead of being caught in the story of the mind – you witness it and it shows itself to you quite clearly. It shows itself to you.

So that's always the beginning. The beginning is always seeing.

~

S: I always hear you talk about being in the presence of an awakened being, which is difficult here, because I live in a very conservative place, and if there are some, I think they would be unknown, because being awake and sharing the Truth would put you in trouble. What do you recommend for people like me, who are looking for an awakened being? Is it enough to attend Satsangs with you online?

V: I understand what you're saying. Fortunately, we have the internet nowadays so you can find awakened teachers online and if they're awakened there will be a presence coming through the transmission.

The seeker has to seek out the teacher. When I was a seeker in Australia, in the 80s, I had to leave Australia. There was no one here who I could sit with. I had to go and live in India and America, and England and Italy, because there was no one here. I think it's always been difficult. Unless you're fortunate enough to be in the same neighbourhood as someone who's awake and who's available. But if you really are a seeker, you'll find your way.

~

S: After I came to your teaching, along with other masters on YouTube, I started having some experiences. Many times, I saw myself as an entity being watched from just awareness, but that only lasted for seconds. After that happened, I started figuring out that I'm not what I used to think I am. That made me more interested in higher consciousness. What are your comments on this and is this what you call satori?

V: It might be satori or it might simply be you being the witness of your own mind. I recall back in the 80s, when I first started meditating, I found no-mind and recognised that, well, I was here, but the mind wasn't here. I was simply witnessing, but the mind wasn't here and that alerted me to the fact that I'm not the mind.

There's something else here and that is when I became very interested in what was going on because up until that point, I thought I was the mind and the body. Then in no-mind, in meditation, in no-mind, I saw I'm here, but there's nobody here. There are no thoughts here, but I'm here. This was seen afterwards. It wasn't seen at the time, it was seen afterwards. I was there, I was present, there was nobody there and there was nobody thinking, and so if the mind is not thinking the mind is not who I am, what am I really? And then the quest to discover my true nature began – the quest to discover that that is aware.

~

S: Why am I unable to get rid of a few old habits?
V: If someone put a gun to your head, you'd probably be able to do it – just not enough motivation. People like to say, well, I have no choice. I have to do this. I have to do that. Oh yeah? If someone put a gun to your head, I wonder what you'd do.

It's all a matter of willpower or discipline, isn't it really? If you're unwilling, well, nothing's gonna change. If you're willing, everything's possible. It's up to you. Bad habits, yeah, if we don't want to give up our bad habits, we won't. If we really want to give them up, we will. It's up to you. Don't ever become a victim of yourself.

~

S: How do you have conversations with others and remain awake, especially at work? How do I not let the ego take over when in these situations? I'm a high school teacher.
V: Okay, so I love what Ramana Maharshi said about self-inquiry. He was asked, when do you stop self-inquiry? And his answer was pretty simple: when there's no one left to inquire. In awakening, you find yourself as Beingness and eventually the "I" is gone.

There is no one left to inquire. There's no point of it coming back either. It's gone.

You're still practising. Keep practising, keep self-inquiring, and keep turning awareness back to itself until there's no one there to come back – until the false one is so seen through that it doesn't have any potential anymore. Keep self-inquiring. This methodology of Ramana Maharshi's works, but it has to be done. It can't be thought about. You can't think it's a good idea and think that somehow that's going to change things. It has to be practised. Anything to do with higher consciousness has to be practised. Collecting knowledge about the subject is probably a waste of time. Practice is what works.

~

S: From your experience, do you need to stay at the so-called "razor's edge" of Enlightenment for a particular length of time to help the Enlightenment process or to make it more solid?

V: The answer to this question is difficult because I don't really know. I know for myself I sat still for nearly six months, 18-hours-a-day after awakening. I felt that that was needed at the time, but I really don't know if that was true. I just did it. I don't know if it was true that I needed to do it or not, and so I can't really honestly answer your question.

My mind was in service to Truth, and in being in service to Truth, it just went quiet. For six months, it just allowed itself to be quiet, to rest in Beingness. Then a teacher came along, one of my teachers came along and brought me out and said "You need to be in the world more" so there was a coming out. By that time there wasn't any "I" left, there was just such a profound nothingness here.

So I don't know the answer to the question. I do know this: the mind itself, particularly the identified part of the mind, needs to become a servant of Truth, and the deal that I found that works best was "Everything for Truth and nothing for you". You give your life to Truth. The false one drops.

~

S: So from the point of awakening, does surrender continue to deepen?

V: I wouldn't say that. Surrender is a non-doing, so when we talk about it deepening, how do you deepen a non-doing? I don't think that's a possibility. Surrender of the self is a non-doing and we learn surrender from the mind's perspective, by practising let-go and acceptance, because that's how you learn to surrender. Let-go and acceptance, and the more you practise let-go and the more you practise acceptance, the better you are at it. It's up to you. What do you practice?

~

S: How do you learn to find the frequency of an awakened teacher or person?

V: Go and sit with them. Go and sit with them and sit as close as you possibly can. If you can't feel them, stay with them because they are definitely putting out a Buddha field. If you can't feel it, it's because you're too closed, not because they're not putting it out. If you stay in the presence of someone who's awake long enough, the defence systems that stop you from feeling will break down and you will start feeling. Go and sit with someone who's awake as close as you possibly can. It'll be just a matter of time before you feel them, if you can't in the beginning. The energy from someone who's awake is palpable. Find someone to sit with who's awake, sit as close as you can, for as long as you can, and see what happens.

~

S: How did you overcome the fear of the unknown of Enlightenment to wake up?
V: Same as I overcame every other fear: by allowing myself to die. See, the ultimate fears are the fear of death, the fear of insanity, and the fear of losing control. If you can find a way to be okay with them then fear has no power over you anymore. What you're doing is surrendering to the outcome that you're frightened of –completely surrendering to the outcome, just making it absolutely 100 per cent okay. In that acceptance of death, in that acceptance of insanity, in that acceptance of losing control, you're free. You're free of fear. It has no power over you anymore because you're not resisting it. Fear gains its power through resistance. Try it and see, see what happens. See what happens when you make the worst okay.

~

S: Is there any trace of the ego left after Enlightenment?
V: Yes, there is a trace. Otherwise, it would be very difficult to communicate and co-operate in the material

world. So when someone calls your name, you turn. That's a form of identification. Ego is just the identified mind. Say the ego is the size of an elephant, and in a lot of people, it is. What's left in someone who's awake is the elephant's tail and that is all. But if the elephant's tail is fed, the ego can come back. It's best not to feed the elephant's tail. There is a trace, and that trace is only there when they're out in the material world. Once they go inside, once the eyes are shut, it's over. There is no ego whatsoever, just . . . just nothingness . . . vast, vast nothingness. To navigate the material world, a little bit of ego, the tail of the elephant, is required.

~

S: Has any part of your mind changed after your awakening?

V: [LAUGHTER] Has any part changed? A lot of the personality is probably still the same. The acumen of the mind is not as good. The business acumen is not as good because the mind is not being used, so it's atrophied in some ways. It's the old story: if you don't use it, you lose it. The energy field of awakening, the Buddha field that's produced, blows the mind apart. The mind just rests in Beingness, rests in the beauty, profoundly content for no reason. It has changed a bit personality-wise, but not that much. Whatever you wake up with is likely to stay. There's not much input impetus, if any, to change anything after awakening. Everything is accepted as it is. No matter how much people complain.

~

S: Could you please talk about the acceptance of our feelings, the process throughout? How to recognize it's happened?

V: Okay, so feelings are just another part of the mind. What's aware of those feelings? What's witnessing those feelings is of interest. Feelings, like thoughts, come and go. What's witnessing them? This is of more interest. There's nothing wrong with feelings as there's nothing wrong with thoughts, but what's witnessing? From the mind's perspective, feelings appear and you can accept them. In the acceptance, everything's okay. They go, they don't stay, they come and they go. What's aware of them? What's this that is purely aware of those feelings and the thoughts that may accompany them? That's of interest. If all we do is get interested in feelings and analysing feelings, understanding feelings, then we're still caught in the mind, we're still caught in a dream. What's aware of those feelings? What's the witness of those feelings? This is of more interest to the seeker.

One of the greatest traps that a seeker can get involved in is analysing the mind thinking that somehow they're raising their consciousness levels. The moment you move to analysing, judging, correcting, you're actually once again dreaming. Dreaming is lower consciousness. Remain the witness. Just watch the mind. See what it does. Don't get caught in collecting knowledge. It won't raise your consciousness levels at all. Simply witness the mind. If anything, the mind needs to surrender, just let it go, let go, let go, that's all. Everything is okay as it is.

~

S: I know people who have had awakening experiences and who now think that they are awake. How does the seeker who gets stuck like this progress?

V: I understand. I had awakening experiences in 1987 and I thought for a little while that I was awake because I was holding the memory of the satoris. But it became really clear to me that the ego was just holding the memory. If you've got a friend or you've had awakenings and you think you're awake, go find someone who's awake to sit with. They'll sort you out very quickly. You see, if you're awake, you're going to have a presence and you're also not going to be there. Go and sit in front of someone who's awake and see. See what happens. Beingness can't be touched by anything, but an ego pretending to be Beingness can be torn apart.

~

S: Why is it that sometimes the more someone's consciousness increases the less progress they seem to have made?

V: As you raise your consciousness levels you get to see the dark side. You get to see all of the things that are failing in you, all of the darkness in you, so it's not that you're going backwards, you're just seeing more. In fact, you're going forwards, you're becoming more and more and more conscious, but as your consciousness rises, you get to see that you're not such a nice person after all. You get to see the good, the bad and the ugly of the psyche, and the pain body starts to appear because you're opening up. Whatever you've repressed comes to the surface and it feels like you might be going backwards, but you're not going backwards. You're emptying out the house. You're clearing the house of a whole pile of rubbish that needs to go. You're not going backwards, you're just opening up and clearing out. This is good. This is what needs to happen.

~

S: Did it ever feel like you were going insane when you started to wake up?

V: In witnessing the mind, I recognised that insanity was already there. Have a look at this. If you believe you're a somebody who's not real and the "I" is not real, that's delusional in itself. The definition of insanity is to think you're a somebody when you're not. The somebody who you think you are, the ego, is based on past memory projected to the future and a whole pile of belief systems. Take away your imagination and that somebody, that "I", doesn't exist. It's delusional. So what is insanity? The only sanity I found was knowing self as Truth, nothing else.

~

S: How can I put my attention on Enlightenment when I'm a busy mum with so much to do?

V: It's possible, but only if you put Truth first. What do you put first? Whatever you put first is where all your awareness is going to go and it's where you're going to live. We can be in the marketplace and put our awareness on Truth. As long as we make Truth first, it'll stay there. The moment we make something else first, there's a potential of it leaving. It comes down to what does the mind actually serve? Does it serve Truth or does it serve itself? In service of Truth,

Enlightenment stays. In service of self, as "I", well, you live as ego-based reality. It's simple. What do you put first? What do you serve? Have a look and see.

~

S: When you say to put Truth first, what does that mean or look like?

V: For someone who's just finding Truth itself, it means keeping awareness on awareness. Not getting caught in distraction, not getting caught in resistance, keeping awareness on awareness. That's what it takes. Whatever we put our awareness on is where we're going to live. If awareness is on itself, well basically you're living as Truth. If awareness is on the mind, and the problems of the mind, well you live as the problems of the mind. Awareness can be in more than one place at a time. It can be on itself and it can also be on the mind, and it can also be on the body and the world. It doesn't necessarily have to be on one place. But for someone who's awake, awareness is always, always on itself, no matter what is happening. The mind becomes a servant of Truth, becomes a servant of love, and in that it puts Truth and love first. It puts itself aside. It sacrifices itself for Truth. This is how awakening stays, if it stays. Who does the mind serve? What does the mind serve? It's up to you. What do you serve?

~

S: Does Enlightenment cause a mutation in the brain cells themselves? Jiddu Krishnamurti and Osho have spoken about the effects of Enlightenment. Is this an indication to know whether Enlightenment has occurred?

V: If Enlightenment has occurred, it can't possibly be missed. If you think that you can wake up and not know it, you're wrong. It is so vastly different than ego-based reality. There is no comparison whatsoever. In ego-based reality, there is a somebody that has reference points. In Being-based reality, there is not a somebody – there is an absence. You can't make the mistake of thinking they're anything alike, because they're not. In ego-based reality, you're basically a single point looking outwards. There's an us-and-a-them kind of feeling. In Being-based reality, there is just "us" as everything. There is a sense of being everything. There is a sense of being connected to everything and there is no sense of separation. We are one. The difference between ego-based reality and Being-based reality is quantum. There is no connection.

~

S: As you began waking up, were there particular obstacles or instances that would bring you back into lower consciousness or ego-based reality?

V: Yes, awakening started in 1998 and about a year later in 1999 awakening was complete in that there was no going back to ego-based reality. During that period, there would have been a thousand or two thousand satoris, flip-flopping from ego-based reality to Being-based reality and back again and what was bringing me back to ego-based reality was basically the non-service of Truth. My mind hadn't completely given itself to Truth yet. It still wanted something for itself. It took a year, to actually fully understand that there's nothing in it for you as an "I".

You have to surrender completely. You give your life to Truth in unconditional surrender and this works. Nothing else works. You can't have anything for you.

Enlightenment does not include you as an "I" because you are a dream, you're not even real. The mind supports awareness aware of itself. You might lose everything. You don't know. You have no idea what's going to happen, but you have to be okay with that. The mind tries to hold on to things. It wants Enlightenment for itself. That's not possible. The mind doesn't get enlightened. Awareness becomes aware of itself. That that's aware of the mind becomes aware of itself. The mind never becomes enlightened. The "I" never becomes enlightened. It can't. It's not even real. It's actually a figment of your own imagination.

So thousands of times, it was a flip-flopping back and forward, knowing self as Truth, knowing self as ego, back and forth, until the mind decided to surrender completely unconditionally and give itself to Truth. Another way of putting that is the mind gives itself to God completely.

~

S: Vishrant, when you encounter an individual, do you know how close they are to Enlightenment? If so, how?

V: I don't know how close they are to Enlightenment, but I do know how advanced they are consciously because I can feel them. When someone's very conscious, they're empty. There's not much there. There's just a whiff of the ego. They've done the work. They've removed a lot of the obstacles. When someone's still in lower consciousness there's a solid feeling about them. It can be felt quite clearly. You come near someone who's awake and you won't feel anything, you won't feel anybody there. You will feel an absence. You'll feel the presence and an absence, but with people who are ego-based, you just feel this solidness. And the more in lower consciousness a person is, the more solidness is there. As people become more conscious, they become less than. There's less there. If there's more silence about them, more stillness about them, more openness about them, there's less of a banging into their stuff and more of a falling into, because there's nothing there. You come and sit next to someone who's awake and you can fall into them because there's just nothing there. It's gone. Awareness is aware of itself. The "I" is just gone. There's no resistance to life anymore, so there's nothing to bang into. It's very beautiful. I remember when I first noticed it with teachers I could get physically close to, I'd start to fall into them. It was a very funny feeling, falling into someone rather than banging into them.

~

S: What were the effects of Enlightenment in terms of your body? Do you become more fragile and loose with existence?

V: The answer to that would be yes, but there was no real movement in becoming more sensitive to everything. There was no movement away. Not really. Everything was okay. It was more painful to be in the world from the perspective of the physical body, because all of the defences are dropped and everything was being felt, but it didn't matter because it was totally accepted. It was like my skin was peeled off and I could feel everything and everybody. Humans carry so much pain and it pours in because energy tends to flow from full to empty. I found it very painful to be in the presence of humans, but it didn't matter. I loved them. Humans carry so much suffering. They collect pain, they repress it, and when they come into the presence of someone who's awake, in the opening, the pain starts to pour out. The pain body starts to pour out. This is just how it is. Everything's okay. There's no resistance.

~

S: I think sometimes I get confused with different types of Enlightenment. Is this kundalini? Or is the paradox of reality taking a hold of you?

V: There's only one type of Enlightenment. There are many different methodologies towards Enlightenment, but there's only one type of Enlightenment. You know yourself as truth or you do not. Enlightenment is knowing self as Truth. In other words, Truth aware of itself or consciousness aware of itself or awareness aware of itself – there aren't two types of Enlightenment, but there are many methodologies towards Enlightenment. They all actually demand surrender. The surrender of mind is the key. There's only one type of Enlightenment, and when you meet someone who's enlightened, the presence will be the same as everybody else's presence who is enlightened. It's like, you go to the ocean, and you find that it's salty. You go to any ocean and you find it is salty. The same with Enlightenment. The Buddha field is always the same. There aren't two different types of Buddha fields. Someone who's awake has awareness on awareness or consciousness aware of itself and has a Buddha field around them. That's the only way that you can tell they're awake actually, but it's always the same, though there are many methodologies towards that, all demanding surrender at some point.

~

S: Osho said that when he became enlightened, there was only a very thin thread to his body and that he hovered around his body. Can one prepare the body for Enlightenment?

V: Yes. What happened for me is I spent the previous 10 years, 12 years, putting awareness into my body so awareness was grounded in the body. If the grounding is not in the body and Enlightenment occurs, there is quite a potential for the person to die. Awareness leaves the body completely. I didn't know why, but I intuitively had many, many practices of putting awareness into the body, into my hands, into my feet, into my legs, and even to this day, after 22 years of Enlightenment, if you were to shake my hand, you can feel the energy is in my hand. Awareness is in the body. It is not out of the body. I think it's important for people who want to wake up to have awareness in the body. I think if there isn't any awareness in the body, the body can get quite sick if it's not taken care of properly. And really, the body is simply a spacesuit with an on-board computer that is not you. You are that that's purely aware of that. When that becomes aware of itself and moves out of the body, the potential is for the body to die, so I think it's important to have grounding of awareness in the body, as well as in Beingness.

~

S: The chemicals in the brain come and go, creating feelings and motivation. Does discipline to awaken really fall within the ability of the mind and personality that is not even real?

V: Sure, it's a pattern. Like any other pattern, you're either disciplined or you're not disciplined, depending on how you've trained the mind. If your mind has been trained to be disciplined, it will be disciplined. If it is not trained to be disciplined, it will not. It's up to you. Have you trained your mind to be disciplined or have you not? A meditator trains the mind to be disciplined, to stay with what is real. In most cases, it's just the breath, but it is real, and the discipline or the program pattern is to stay with the breath, stay with what is real, and not deviate. That takes practice. I mean, we all went to school so we will have been disciplined or trained to be still, sitting in class, not walk around and not interfere. We've all been trained and disciplined to some degree. It's up to you. It's just a pattern. What patterns have you produced? Or what patterns have you not? A disciplined mind will support Enlightenment. An undisciplined mind probably won't. Have a look.

~

S: You say you will fall into the awakened one. I have the experience that I'm falling into my own presence. Please comment.

V: Ahah! Which are you? The presence or the one falling? What's aware is more relevant really. What's aware? Always, what is witnessing this? This is relevant. Everything else is just an experience appearing in who you are, and people get lost in looking at the experience. What's aware? What's the witness of what's happening? This is more relevant.

~

S: If the Buddha field is the same from enlightened masters, is it possible to love two teachers at the same time? It almost feels like having two lovers, that the experience of being in both of their presences is the same pure love and Truth.

V: In the absence of the "I" – which is the main obstacle – in the absence of the "I", everything and everyone is loved, so when you ask is it possible to love two masters, how about loving everybody and everything? As the "I" disappears more and more, that is absolutely possible. All prejudices disappear, all defence systems disappear, and there is just openness. In that openness, everything is loved. The only reason people have trouble loving more than one thing is because they're closed. They're cut off in the adventure towards Enlightenment. All of those closures, all of those defences are removed so those who are awake love all.

~

S: Can pain be grounding?

V: Our pain is very grounding because when you're putting your awareness in the body long enough, it locks in. What ungrounds people is putting awareness on the mind and just on the mind, and then you're grounded in something that's not real. There's nothing real about the mind. It's imagined. So being grounded in the mind is dangerous. Being grounded in the body is quite healthy because it's real. Being grounded in Beingness is better because it's ultimately real. It is the ultimate reality, pure awareness, that that we are, that that is everything and is always here, being grounded, and that's always best. That's Enlightenment.

~

S: It feels as if practising acceptance and surrender constantly becomes exhausting yet usually ends in satori. Other times, effortless witnessing meditation seems to end in satori as well. Is this normal?

V: My answer is really simple. Whatever works is worthy. I'm totally pragmatic. Whatever works for you is the right way to go for you. I love self-inquiry. I love meditation. I love witnessing the mind. I love the practice of openness. But whatever works for you. Whatever opens you up, whatever shows you truth is worthy. There are many paths. Whatever works is best. My understanding is that if you're really interested in Enlightenment, find someone who's awake and have them guide you because the ego is such a tricky creature. It's more than a million years old and it's amazing at finding ways to survive, and really it is in its unconditional surrender that Enlightenment is supported. When you find someone who's awake to sit with, they'll help you with that. It's best. It's always best. Find someone who's awake and sit with them.

Thank you for Satsang, good to see bravehearts here today.

CHAPTER FOUR

Love and Gratitude

S: Can you please speak about the topic: Love and Gratitude?
V: Love is real, what you think is not, so even words in a way don't have the same reality that true love has. Love is a mystery to me, because it's here and it's always here. It's perceived, but it doesn't do anything else but love. Sometimes it's referred to as the true jewel of consciousness and it was because of this unconditional love that is here, that is real, that my whole life changed. There was a recognition that it was worthy – that it was worthy of pursuit, and that materialism and just the pursuit of happiness, or escaping suffering, didn't have the same worthiness.

So I had to discover how to perceive more love because my mind really liked it, and through experimentation, I discovered that love was present when I as an "I" was absent. The less "I", the more love. And as I looked at that I saw that the "I" is quite a defensive thing. It's quite a resistant thing, and all resistance and all defensiveness, all closures block our view, block our perception of love. For a lot of years of my life I didn't really perceive real love because I was too closed. In discovering real love, unconditional love, I went in pursuit of more of it, because I liked the sample I got.

In that pursuit I took down all of the defence systems and I opened up, and in that openness, the "I" starts to diminish, because the "I" itself is a form of closure. The less story there was of Vishrant, the more love there was.

Quite often people project on to love all sorts of things. They think somehow it talks to them. But love just loves. It doesn't talk. It's the mind that thinks and talks. And it's the mind that projects all of these things onto love, thinking that somehow it can control love, but how can something that's not even real, that's imagined, actually control something that is real? Not really. All the mind can do is get out of the way enough so love can be perceived. And when love is perceived, when the mind is experiencing unconditional love, it just wants to take care of everyone and everything. It doesn't need rules anymore. It doesn't need morality anymore because it will do no harm.

And this is one of the beautiful aspects of finding unconditional love in your life. It affects you in such a lovely way where you just want to take care, where you just want to support, where you will do anything to help people out of their suffering, if you can. You'll become God's fool, using humour to take people out of their seriousness so they can drop their defences and find something of beauty.

The path of love is the path of least resistance, and when we look at that, we go, "Well, how much resistance do we put into life? How much do we defend ourselves? How closed are we?" And in seeing, we can start to open up. We can start to drop our defences. We can start walking through the world vulnerable instead of defended, instead of closed. And in that vulnerability, love is perceived, the beauty is perceived. Love changes your life. It changes your life so dramatically.

I have a story about it, which is interesting because it did change my life dramatically. This is a long time ago back in 1987. I had taken a small boat with my girlfriend over to the Abrolhos Islands which are about 35 miles (58km) off the west coast of Australia and I hadn't checked the weather. It was a very small boat, about 15 feet, (4.5m) with a high-powered motor on it. As I took off, the weather started to change, but I wasn't paying attention to it and within half an hour, a cyclone had hit.

The islands at their highest point are only 10 feet (3m) high, and I went straight through them, missed them, ending up 60 miles (96km) off the coast in this run-about at the edge of a cyclone. On the way through somewhere, we hit something in the water, maybe a bottle or something, and it holed the first hull. So at 60 miles (96km) out, the boat started to sink. And it sunk. It went down below gunnel level. We had a radio attached to the roof, fortunately with batteries, and we were able to talk to people, but we were in the water and it didn't look good because we were being circled by sharks for 18 hours.

I thought at that time that I wouldn't survive and that my partner would die as well, probably from being mauled by sharks. At some point, as I looked across to her, this unconditional love that was non-directional just appeared. It was so beautiful. It was so special. I realised that everything that I had, that I'd earned up to that age – I was 33, I think – was worthless, except this love, except this beauty. I had been a successful publisher in Perth driving a Rolls Royce. I had houses, properties, a thriving business, but none of it was worth anything. In that moment, the only thing that was worth anything was love.

And I valued it. Within nine months of that experience, I decided to give away my business and to pursue Heart, to pursue love, because I realised that for 33 years, I had selfishly lived my life for me and it was a waste because the only thing that's valuable on this plane is love. I walked into my publishing company and gave the company to my staff, not wanting to see them put out by me selling it. I gave them the company and left the business world and basically hitchhiked around Australia for the next four years, looking for my Heart.

It took me a while to work out where it was and what it was. I didn't realise that I couldn't find it while I was defended, while I was closed or resisting life. I didn't realise at that stage. It took a fair bit of looking to see that when I was really vulnerable, when I was really open, there love was, and it was always here, it was just out of perception. If I was closed, if I was defended, if I was resisting life, my awareness would be on that, and be blocked by those filters.

In finding Heart, I discovered what I wanted to do with my life. I didn't want to be a businessman anymore. I wanted to be in service to humans because when Heart affects the mind you just want to help people. So I went back to school and I trained as a naturopath and as a psychotherapist to have some tools to help people with. It was so rewarding to love – to truly, truly love – without anything, to experience the magnificence of unconditional love. I teach the Way of the Heart because I know what it's worth. It's worth everything. But it's up to you to take down your defences. It's up to you to stop resisting life. It's up to you to open up because love is always here.

Any questions, any statements, any challenges to this teaching today?

S: Is it true that everything is love?

V: Well, I don't know. It could be. I have experienced everything as love. Many, many, many times, but I don't know if it's true. I find that the best answer for most questions like that is "I don't know" because like everybody else, I have a limited mind and existence is so big. So asking, "Is everything love?" I just know I know that love is real. I know that love is the true jewel of consciousness and I know that if you find love in your life, you have a beautiful life.

~

S: When you say love makes you take care of others, is worrying a form of care?

V: It can be. It can be deemed that way. But worrying itself is a form of closure, which cuts you off from love. It's a filter that we put on, that actually is in resistance to what is because we're fearful of something happening, and in that resistance, we actually cut ourselves off from love. It might be love that motivates us in the first place to worry, but once we start worrying, we're in resistance. The perception of love, the true perception of love has probably disappeared. Love really does appear in openness. Closure tends to cut us off from perceiving it and worrying is a form of closure.

~

S: How does unconditional love compare to the experience of things like MDMA?

V: MDMA, ecstasy, is a drug that can effectively knock the ego out temporarily by overwhelming it. An amphetamine-based drug can have people experiencing love. In the early days, it was called the love drug, and that was because of the amount of amphetamine that had been taken or MDMA that had been taken knocking the ego out, knocking out the mind's defences so love could be perceived. That works temporarily, but then the mind comes back with a vengeance afterwards to defend itself because it doesn't like being knocked out.

If you really want to find unconditional love, without taking drugs, learn to let go, learn to open up and learn to accept life. All the drug does is open you up because you're closed. Find the things that are keeping you closed and remove them, and then that beautiful experience of love that you may find very temporarily on ecstasy is there all the time. Anything that forces the mind open is going to get a reaction from the mind so maybe people experience a little bit of love on the first few trips of ecstasy, MDMA, but after a while the mind has defended itself against being knocked out because after all it is a survival mechanism.

You can teach the mind to let go. You can teach the mind to be undefended. You can teach the mind to open up. And if you do, you're putting yourself in the right position to experience unconditional love.

~

S: I've heard it said that you can't love another until you first love yourself. What is your perspective on this?

V: That's an idea, not a reality. If you're out of the picture, love is there, you know, if you're out of the picture. Now what takes you out of the picture? If you're undefended, if you're open, love can be there and you can perceive it.

As far as loving yourself is concerned, unless you're in full acceptance of yourself, it is relatively difficult to love yourself because there's a part of your mind at odds with another part of your mind. There's a little disjointedness inside of your own mind with one part judging another part and holding it in contempt in some way. Not accepting ourselves creates low self-worth and that is one of the main things creating resistance in us and stopping us from perceiving love.

So it's important for the seeker to find a way to accept themselves as they are – the good, the bad and the ugly, and to hold themselves in tenderness. In that tenderness, love can be perceived. As you become more loving with yourself as a result of being more accepting of yourself, you start to overflow and you become an oasis of love for others. This is beautiful. You become the heart of gold that you've been looking for, but that's up to you. The more defended you are, the more closed you are, the more resistant you are, the more difficult that's going to be.

It's up to you. Always up to you.

~

S: I often watch my mind contracting when people close to me don't have the same world views, for example about abortion, but I still love and serve them where I can although with some reservation and holding back. How do I just let it be in love?

V: Well, you're talking about having points of view. You're talking about having opinions that are keeping you separate from others. Drop the opinions, drop the judgments and just be open. Then you'll find that you love everybody. That level of prejudice in the opinions and judgments that you strongly support is a form of resistance that will stop you from perceiving love. You're creating it. Nobody's doing it to you. You create your reality by the way you think and you can change that if you like because you're in charge.

~

S: You say that love affects the mind to want to take care. Does love also have a feeling in the body?

V: It may do, I just can only talk from the experience that I have with love. Love is everywhere, so it's not in the body, it's everywhere. It's not directional, it's omnipresent. It's everywhere. So to say it's in the body would be too difficult for me. It's everywhere.

S: So if love is not an emotional body sensation, are other feelings everywhere too?

V: Love is not an emotion. Love is real. People can get emotional when they experience love which is a part of the mind, but love itself is not an emotion. It just is, and it's very, very beautiful and the mind perceives it as such. It is the mind that gets emotional. It's the mind that thinks, but the mind isn't that real. If you take away imagination, there is no mind. But love on the other hand is real, it is here, it is not imagined. [LAUGHTER] So beautiful! Just get out of the way enough to feel it. Sometimes when people come in touch with a newborn baby, they feel that love because they're totally undefended in the presence of the baby. They're totally open, and in that openness, they experience love.

This is the way to live. This is the Way of the Heart. This is the true rebellion, if you like, because this goes against the mind's survival mechanism. This sets you free from that. The Way of the Heart in a lot of ways demands that you abandon a lot of what you think. You abandon the things that contract you. You abandon your defence systems. You abandon anything that causes resistance in yourself. This is a rebellion against your own mind, for the Heart. This is the true rebellion.

~

S: How can I discern if I'm experiencing love or attachment to my partner?
V: Let them go and see. Allow them to leave and see. Be alone and see. See what's holding you. See what's really there. Love doesn't take prisoners ever. The mind does because it wants to feel secure, so the mind takes prisoners, but love never does.

~

S: If you practise gratitude, does being loving naturally follow?

V: No, not necessarily. You can practise gratitude and still be closed unfortunately. If you practise gratitude, and you're open, yeah, I'd say that you probably perceive love, but gratitude can be practised from a closed space. Gratitude has the potential to open you up, but it's not the only thing that's required. You actually have to watch your mind and see what it is that keeps you closed, what defences might be in play. A lot of those may be unconscious, so you have to look very closely. You have to watch your mind and see what it's doing. It's up to you.

~

S: I would like to ask about when you are in love with someone like a boyfriend or girlfriend, in those moments, how you can keep aware of yourself? When you're in love, it is like a dream. Do I have to be aware in that position? Can you just guide me through please?

V: Well, "in love" is a funny expression: you're in love with someone. Love is there and you can experience love and then blame someone else for it and say I love you. Really, if you have a look, love is real and the "I" is not. It's just imagined. So when we look at loving people, a lot of what we call love is actually not love. It's bonding that happens chemically out of need and out of insecurities. We quite often call that love, but it's more need than love. Love can be there, but not necessarily.

True love doesn't want anything in return ever. It doesn't take prisoners. It just is. The primal bonding that we get when we mate with someone or we're attached to them in some way is a little different, and to be able to tell the difference you have to start witnessing your own mind and see what it's really up to. One thing about love is it never ever, ever gets attached to anything. It just is. It just loves. If there's attachment there, there's something else there. You have a look and see. What is it that's really there? Is it absolutely pure love, or is there something else going on?

~

S: When you were talking about loving a baby, I really felt the truth of that. Recently a friend of mine who's in his late 40s came to the door with a beautiful little baby in his arms. As I was looking at the baby, he said, "I wish I had a camera to photograph every time somebody looks at the baby and goes like that."

V: It's simple because babies are harmless, the same as puppies are harmless, the same as kittens are harmless. We don't defend ourselves when we're near them, so because we're not defended, we perceive love. The moment we're with an adult human being or a child that's a little bit older than a year, a certain level of defensiveness comes up because humans are dangerous, and in that defensiveness, we don't perceive the love because we're actually closed and we don't even know it.

S: I can hear what you're saying because that is my experience when I'm with babies or young kids. Two-year-olds are also really beautiful. One of the reasons I don't watch TV and I don't read newspapers is when

I see all the negative stuff that's going on with the people that are harming other people I contract. I think it was the Dalai Lama once said, "It's okay to hate the sin, but try to love the sinner," but why do I find that so difficult?

V: Well, if you take away your defence systems you can love everybody. The only reason you can't love people is because you've got something against them, you're holding a defence system. You're holding something in resistance to them. If you drop all resistance – which quite often happened when people used to take massive doses of ecstasy – you love everybody and everything, but that's because all of the defences, all the resistances have been removed and there love is, you know. People thought that ecstasy created the love. Ecstasy never created love. Amphetamine never created love. Love is always here. It's just not being perceived because we're closed, because that's part of our survival mechanism to be closed, to be resistant. The Way of the Heart is against nature in some ways because it means we have to be open and vulnerable, which is against survival.

S: Yeah, again, I totally understand what you're saying. I guess the thing for me is I've gotten into such a habit of being judgmental, including of myself, that I find it difficult. But thanks for sharing that. I'm gonna really keep trying to work on it.

V: You know I love you.

S: I know and I love you too Vishrant, but it's easier to love you than Donald Trump.

V: Ah, you know, I love Donald Trump. I don't agree with some of the things he's done or said, but I love him. He's just another part of me the same as you are.
S: Yeah, we've got to love everybody warts and all.
V: Pretty much, otherwise we live in a closed, cut-off world, and that's not happy. That's miserable.

It's nice to talk to you.

~

S: In the last interaction you were responding that it is good to love everybody, and you said pretty much. It sounded like there might be times when it's okay not to. I guess I'm talking more about acceptance of how somebody is. Is acceptance and love the same thing?
V: No, acceptance is what the mind does. Love is independent of the mind. Love is real. Acceptance is still part of the mind. But a mind that is in acceptance is likely to perceive love. A mind that is in non-acceptance is not likely to perceive love.
S: Yes, and one other thing you said earlier was that you don't feel love in the body necessarily. I tend to. I tend to have a real resonance when I touch that, when I let go of everything else and just be and just love. So it is kind of visceral as well. It is a full feeling.
V: I just . . . it's everywhere. I tend to be, awareness tends to be, located everywhere. Yeah, I can't put a place or pin a place where awareness is. It's all. It's everywhere.
S: Yes, thank you.
V: It's nice to talk to you.
S: Oh, yes so good, thank you.

~

S: The next question: Is this love like experiencing the Buddha field?

V: You can experience love in a Buddha field, but a Buddha field is created by awareness being aware of itself or consciousness being aware of itself in a human being. Then there's a Buddha field, and that is the True Buddha, the Buddha field. Love can appear in that, but not necessarily. So once again, we start entering the mystery of it all. The Buddha field is beautiful, and love can be in it, but not necessarily.

~

S: When you said earlier, in reference to Donald Trump, that he's just another part of you, how do you come to experience this in the moment when seeing all of the negative things he has done?

V: Yeah. You have to be awake. You have to be enlightened. The funny thing about that is it's not you that becomes enlightened, it's not the mind that becomes enlightened, it's not the ego that becomes enlightened. That that's aware of your mind discovers itself and becomes aware of itself, pure consciousness becomes aware of itself, which is nonpersonal. In that awareness of self, there is the mind knowing that everything is one and that there is no such thing as duality at all. We are all one. So Donald Trump or anyone else, or anything else, is just another part of us. That's not held as a concept. It's held as a direct knowing from the direct experiencing of it in the moment.

~

S: The next question: When I'm stressed about something not going how I want, how can I see that I'm lucky to have this present moment and be grateful for what I have?

V: Don't give yourself a choice. We have choices to go negative on something or positive on something or not get involved at all. We have choices. Life is just the way it is. We don't have to see it as good or bad. We can just say "This is what is" and if we can say "This is just what is," we don't need to go into story either. Because the moment we accept life as it is, story disappears, drama disappears. And this is quite beautiful. It's up to you though. How does your mind work? Why does it work? What is it doing? By witnessing the mind, we get to see that. And as we witness the mind more and more and see how it's operating, there's certain things we just don't get involved in anymore because they're detrimental. Life is just the way it is.

~

S: Did gratitude arise in you spontaneously or did you actively practise it?

V: No, it arose spontaneously. I first noticed it to a level where it was bringing tears to my eyes when I thought about my spiritual master and teacher Osho Rajneesh. I was so overwhelmed with gratitude for what he had shown me, love just appeared. It was so beautiful, but it wasn't something I practised. It was something that just arose spontaneously.

~

S: Is love something that can be taught?

V: Well, you can teach a person to get out of the way. You can teach a person to open up. You can teach a person to stop resisting life. When I say teach, you can offer them teaching, but they're the ones who have to open up. They're the ones who have to drop their defence systems. It's possible for someone to experience love if they're willing to open up. As far as teaching them is concerned, it's a bit like, you can lead the horse to water, but you can't make him drink. It's up to the individual. The whole journey to higher consciousness, the whole perception of love is up to you. You're the only one who can make it so. Nobody can do it for you. No teacher can do it for you. Not really. You have to do it. You have to undo your defence systems and you have to drop your resistances. You have to see through your mind and let things go. Only you can do that.

~

S: Is Heart awakening related in any way to the awakening to Truth?

V: In this way it is. For the Heart to awaken there needs to be a surrender on the part of the mind, and for Enlightenment to occur there needs to be a surrender on the part of the mind, so surrender or unconditional surrender is the key to both. We learn surrender by the practice of acceptance and the practice of let-go, and if we practise acceptance and let-go enough, we master surrender. In that way there is a connection between Enlightenment and awakening of the Heart as they both demand unconditional surrender.

~

S: Do you think that having a daily gratitude practice can help stop negative thinking?

V: It may do. I don't know. I've never tried it. It may do. I don't know. I'm not big on giving anybody anything more to think about, and when we start practising gratitude, we're thinking about more things. I see the mind as something that is best let go of, and be present to what is real instead. That's what I think. That's called meditation. Sometimes it's called mindfulness training. I know that works.

~

S: I'm scared to open up and truly, truly love other people. How can I overcome my fear of being hurt?

V: Yeah, right, well if you open up, you will be hurt because that's what happens. That's one of the prices for serving Heart. There is a willingness to be hurt, there's a willingness to be open, and there's a willingness to be vulnerable. In that vulnerability, yeah, we can get hurt, but that's part of the deal. If you're not willing to comply, if you don't want to open up, if you don't want to feel something, you're creating your reality through that closure. It's up to you.

You say you're frightened. Yeah, of course, it's frightening. It's frightening to be hurt by others, but if we want to serve Heart, if we want to experience love, we have to be willing to feel. Otherwise the closures that we use to protect ourselves from feeling get in the way of us perceiving love. Once again, it's up to you. No one can make you do it. It's up to you.

~

S: How did you become okay with feeling other people's emotional pain? Are you still in ecstasy or love while feeling this pain?

V: It is the strangest thing in the world, when other people's pain comes into me as an energy form – and it usually does if I'm with humans – it turns into ecstasy because of the unconditional surrender here. It turns into bliss. So when I'm in the presence of somebody who's pouring their pain into me, I'm blissed out. I do feel the pain, but there is no resistance to it whatsoever; and in that non-resistance, in that unconditional surrender, there is such nectar. There is so much bliss.

~

S: I'm in non-acceptance of my partner not finding a job. Can love be a tool to help me drop my resistance?

V: Turning love into a tool? I wouldn't do that. Love is just love. It's very beautiful. The reason you don't accept is because your mind doesn't want to accept because it wants something, so it doesn't want to accept what is. If you really want to accept, you accept. Trying to think of using love as a tool, it's a bit ... I don't think so. I don't think so. Find out what it is you're not willing to feel and you'll find the answer. There's something there that you're not willing to feel. Your non-acceptance is there because you don't want to feel something. Find out what it is you want to feel or don't want to feel, and be okay with that and see where that takes you.

~

S: Is gratitude just a high degree of acceptance?

V: I don't know. I really don't know. Gratitude is beautiful. See, a high degree of acceptance is actually surrender and surrender is a non-doing. In gratitude there's still a doing of some kind and so I don't really know. When we learn enough about acceptance, when we practise it enough, when we practise enough let-go, we find surrender. But surrender is a non-doing. Things could happen that might not be savoury, that might not be good, but there's no reaction to it. This is a surrendered mind. Gratitude is still a doing where there's someone who is grateful for something. In unconditional surrender there's actually an absence of the "I". There's an absence of the one who would have gratitude. That's a little bit hard to understand, but it's true. In unconditional surrender there is no "I". It's over.

~

S: Next question is from a viewer. How can you accept a being such as Hitler?

V: Easy, he's part of me. How can I not accept part of me? We all have the good, the bad and the ugly in us, all of us, as far as the psyche of the human is concerned. If you know yourself as Truth, you know yourself as everything and everyone. How can you not accept yourself? How can you be your own enemy? How can you not be your own friend? It may be that you don't agree with parts of yourself, but you accept them anyway. You hold them in tenderness anyway because everything is one.

If you only look at it from the perspective of the ego though, you see the world as separate from you. You live in the world of duality so you think some people are good and some are bad. That perspective is from being an ego which is separate. From the perception of reality, there is no two, there is only one: one totality. In that totality you perceive perfection upon perfection upon perfection, no matter what. But that can't be understood. It can be known, but it can't be understood. Go for Enlightenment. Find yourself as Truth and find this to be true for yourself. I don't want anyone to ever believe anything I'm saying. I want you to find out for yourself. Go for it yourself. Find out what's true for yourself. But you won't find that much that's true inside of the mind. You've got to go beyond the mind to find yourself as pure awareness. And then you'll see.

~

S: You feel other people's emotional pain. Do you also feel people's physical pain?
V: Sometimes. Sometimes I feel their physical pain. Sometimes I feel their headaches.

One of the reasons that I do what I do is because this plane that we live on as human beings tends to be, for human beings at least, a plane of suffering. People are in resistance to life and they suffer a great deal, but we don't need to. We can actually climb above it and know ourselves as Truth and then be a light so others can see. My endeavour is to help people find themselves as Truth so they can be lights for others to see in this realm of suffering.

Become a bodhisattva, that's best.

Thank you for Satsang. Good to see you bravehearts here today.

CHAPTER FIVE

Celebrating Life

S: Hello Vishrant, can you please talk about the topic of celebrating life?
V: Well, there's nothing else to do here really. If you're not celebrating life, what are you doing? After examining the meaning of life for so many years and finding that I couldn't find a meaning, and the only meaning I could find was life itself, well, why not celebrate it? Why not celebrate the fact that we have a body, that we're here, and that it's a gift?

All that is, is an attitude really.

I had this amazing teacher, Osho Rajneesh, who taught celebrating life as a way of living and I agree. I agree totally. I think that's the way we should live. Most people, for one reason or another, tend to problem-solve, so they live in their minds to a large degree during the day problem solving. I don't see that as celebrating. With celebrating life, there's joy, there's bliss, there's happiness. It doesn't mean getting drunk or getting stoned. It means celebrating life, squeezing the juice out of life.

It's probably not until we realise how impermanent we are that we stop wasting our time on things that are mundane. When we start seeing that we're only here for a very short period, why waste any moments in misery? Why not celebrate this life and bring that celebration to other people as well? Include them in it. There are seven-and-a-half billion people on the planet to celebrate with.

I love celebrating life and I love the idea of celebrating life. Finding people to celebrate life with, that's fun too, but it's up to you. It's all attitudinal really, because we create our reality by the way we think.

How does your mind think? Is it always looking for the negative? Is it always looking for the problems in life? Or is it celebrating? It's up to you. You're going to create your reality. Nobody's going to do it to you. Find people to celebrate life with. Squeeze it totally. Make it happen. Make it so.

S: What kind of people do you choose to celebrate life with?

V: Everyone I meet. I don't have a prejudice. I really don't. Everybody is the same, everybody is Beingness. Why have any prejudice whatsoever? Why be sexist? Why be racist? Why be ageist? Why not celebrate life with everybody to whatever degree they are prepared to celebrate life with you? Everybody's there to celebrate life with. It depends on your attitude.

~

S: Did you choose who you hung out with before you were awake?

V: In some ways yes and in some ways no. I was very involved in life before awakening, working as a naturopath and psychotherapist. I had a large client base that I saw daily. I had a group of friends and I had family. I was always surrounded by people in a lot of ways because I love people. I just love people. They're my favourite species. The next favourite is dogs. I love dogs. There are so many people out there to celebrate life with. You can celebrate life by smiling at someone as you walk past them in a mall or on a street. It doesn't have to be so formal.

~

S: Do you think that discipline and celebrating life can go hand in hand?
V: Discipline is a wonderful thing because it gives you a structure to work in. That allows a lot of freedom once you develop it. When we're born, we don't have disciplined minds, we don't have any structure to operate in. And so we can make a lot of mistakes. Having a mind that is relatively disciplined shows us where our boundaries are, shows us how we can play in a way where it doesn't hurt others, where it doesn't hurt ourselves. And so I don't see discipline as in the way of celebrating life at all. I see it as an aid to celebrating life.

~

S: I see my mind as addicted to suffering. I sometimes have resistance to celebrating because of this. How do I move past this?
V: Yes, it's not so much that you're addicted to suffering, it's just become a pattern of life. Usually, it's a result of being victim-orientated, seeing yourself as a victim of situations or people or even of yourself. Then the drama begins because the moment we see ourselves as any form of victim of anything there's drama, and the drama is always miserable. That's

a habit you've developed and it's a habit that can be changed by not entertaining victim orientation, by actually not being negative about life. Really, we're just talking about negativity. We don't need to become positive because humans are naturally buoyant, but if we really want to be happy and we want to celebrate life, we probably need to stop entertaining negativity. So it's up to you whether you do that or not. Have a look at it. What would your life be like if you didn't entertain negativity? If every time a negative thought came up, you just let it go? What would your life be like?

~

S: Sometimes after Satsang, my heart is full of joy and celebration and sometimes a lot of gunk from deep down surfaces, making it hard to celebrate. What should I do?

V: Look, you accept whatever appears. If it's joy, you accept joy. If it's love, you accept love. If it's pain, you accept pain. If it's sadness, you accept sadness. If it's fear, you accept fear. You always begin with acceptance, and you're on the right track. It's the cure-all. It means we're no longer in resistance to life no matter what is happening, but because we're not programmed to accept life, it takes a while for us to learn how to do it. We have to practise it. In the practice we get better at it because we're practising. You can listen to me and think, "Oh, that's a great idea and now you have an insight. Whoo! I'm going to accept life." Well, that's not worth anything unless it's put into practice. It is only in the practice of something different to what you've been doing before that the mind changes its patterns and sometimes that practice needs to be for quite a long time.

If you practise acceptance of life for long enough, it becomes a default pattern, and so there's no longer any need for discipline. It just happens by itself. But that's up to you. What are you going to practise? You're responsible. You create your reality with your way of thinking.

~

S: Isn't there a danger to be lost in the mundane by celebrating life too much?
V: I haven't experienced that, no. I love celebrating life. I remember when I left school, and you know, after people leave school they have a bit of a party, the end of school leavers or whatever they call it, and I remember I celebrated life for another 27 years after that. Why stop? Why stop? Why not celebrate life? I can't think of a good reason really not to celebrate life, the good, the bad, and the ugly, all of it. If you're in acceptance of life, you can celebrate it. It's only when we're not in acceptance of life as it is that we can't celebrate it. Acceptance is the cure-all for everything, and if you practise it, you will get good at it.

~

S: How do you celebrate life with people having negative energy?
V: I can't help myself. I don't know about you, but I'm not affected by what other people think or do. I can't be bothered. What they're doing is their business. Whether they're being negative or positive is

their problem, not mine. Whether they like me or they don't like me is their business, not my business. I'm running my own show and my show includes celebrating life no matter what.

~

S: How is the celebration different pre- and post-awakening?

V: The thing about awakening is it's very, very different because the ego disappears. The mind – the identified mind – disappears. So the patterns that were available as default patterns before Enlightenment will still be running after Enlightenment and if the pattern before Enlightenment was to celebrate life, there's a very good chance that pattern will continue after Enlightenment.

After Enlightenment, the motivation to change anything disappears. Everything's perfect as it is: the good, the bad, and the ugly – the broken is even great. It's all perfect. If you're going to change something about yourself, it's best to change it before awakening.

But in looking back and seeing if there's any difference, there's a huge difference. Before awakening, there was an ego involved in doing everything, and like everyone else's ego, trying to make it work. After awakening, the ego wasn't there. There's just emptiness dancing.

S: What do you mean by emptiness dancing?

V: Well, life is a dance. It's like a great big play, but there's nobody dancing. There's nobody playing. The ego is not real and when awakening occurs it's seen as not real and it drops. It's surrendered. It's gone. The identified one's gone. It's not there. So there's dancing, but there's nobody dancing. There's walking, but there's nobody walking. There's talking, but there's nobody talking. There's sitting, but there's nobody sitting.

~

S: What is the acceptance of life? Should we try to change our lives actively, for instance by trying to get a better job, etc.?

V: Heck, yeah. Why not? Acceptance doesn't preclude changing things. It just means you'll be changing things from a place of openness instead of a place of resistance. Acceptance is brilliant. It just means that you don't have stress anymore. So you win? You win. You lose? You lose. It's all good. You just keep playing. Acceptance is like a lubricant that makes everything run smoothly. And when we don't have acceptance, we get resistance, and in that resistance we suffer. The best thing a human being can learn is acceptance of life because that actually eventually teaches us surrender, and surrender is the key to Enlightenment – unconditional surrender of the mind. You give yourself to Truth without conditions and that works. So acceptance is wonderful.

S: After acceptance, is acting on our desires a celebration of life?

V: Look, from my perspective everything is a celebration of life. I mean, we have this amazing ability to be here. And we're not going to be here for that long. We're terminal. Why not celebrate life? The best way to celebrate life is to find love and we find love by opening right up, by dropping our defences and walking through the world in a vulnerable way. When we find love, when we perceive love, we love everybody: the good, the bad, and the ugly, everyone. We love everyone because love has no prejudice. This is a wonderful way to live. It's up to you. You're the one who's going to create this, or you're the one who is going to create something different than this. We are the masters of our own reality in that we create what we're doing by the way we think.

~

S: Sometimes when I'm really happy around people who are having a hard time, they can seem to get annoyed. Is it the Way of the Heart to tone down my happiness if it is triggering people?

V: Well I must annoy a lot of people and I must have annoyed a lot of people my whole adult life because I like being happy. And if people have a problem with me being happy, that truly is their problem, not my problem. You know what other people think is actually their business, not your business. People make themselves happy or unhappy. You can't do it. No one can make me unhappy and no one can make me happy. I'm responsible for my reality.

People want to be miserable around you because you're so happy, let them be miserable. That's their doing. They're creating that. You're not creating it. You're not doing anything. You're just being you.

S: Does accepting life and being happy mean we are celebrating life?

V: Heck yeah. Why not? Loving life is celebrating life, and if we're open enough, we love life. The only reason that we might not be perceiving love is because somewhere there's a closure, somewhere there's defensiveness. If we're wide open, then love is here. It's always here. And then we celebrate life. Loving life is celebrating life.

~

S: Does awakening lead to better moral decisions?
V: No, the thing about awakening is morality disappears because it belongs to a set of rules that belong to the mind. What replaces it is Heart, and because Heart is present, because love is present, no harm will be done. Everything and everyone will be taken care of because that's how the Heart affects the mind. Those who have Heart don't need morality. Only those who do not have Heart need morality. The Heart is the most beautiful thing in the world and when it affects the mind, the mind just wants to take care of everybody and everything. It will do no harm.

~

S: What is the most important practice I can integrate into my life that will help me to celebrate life?
V: Openness. There is nothing more important than openness. If you can practise openness, you remove all of the obstacles that are in the way of Enlightenment. If you practise openness, you remove all of the obstacles that are in the way of the Heart. If you practise openness, you'll heal all the wounds of the Heart. Openness counts for everything and it's the one thing people don't like to practise. But it's the

one thing the ego cannot use to survive in. Openness, true openness, is without ego. The ego itself is a form of closure. The practice of openness is a way to Enlightenment by itself.

~

S: How can you celebrate life while going through hard times, like poverty or the death of loved ones?
V: I have been through poverty. I have been through the death of loved ones. I can still celebrate life because this is just part of life. To think that something is wrong, to think something is out of place, to think that something is not perfect as it is, is an incorrect understanding of what is. There is nothing but perfection upon perfection upon perfection. The idea of right and wrong is simply an idea. There is just what is, and this deep understanding that life is just the way it is is in itself freedom. The moment we get caught in right, wrong, good and bad, we can take ourselves to hell pretty quickly. In seeing life as this is just what is, we can stay equanimous. This is one of the keys to creating a mind that will support Enlightenment.

Thank you for satsang. Good to see you bravehearts here today.

CHAPTER SIX

Seva

S: Can you please talk about the topic of seva?
V: Seva means service. That's what the word seva means and seva is what happens around monasteries and ashrams where volunteers come in and give their time to help. My understanding of seva goes a great deal further. When we choose to serve Heart, we find that we end up in service in some way, to the planet, to plants, to animals, to human beings, even to cleaning the carpet because the Way of the Heart, how love affects us, makes us want to take care of everyone and everything.

So seva for me is synonymous with the Way of the Heart. If we look at it from the perspective of human relationships, if we're really living the Way of the Heart, we are into serving everybody and everything. We're into serving our partners. And that becomes very beautiful. Instead of trying to get something or take something, we're trying to give something back because this is how love affects our minds. We just want to give, we want to take care. Altruism, which means giving without wanting anything back, is a part of seva. The reward in seva is actually the giving. The reward is the service itself. That's the beauty of that.

And people go "Well, that's a bit hard". But if you really love people, you really love the planet, you really love the trees and the plants, it's beautiful to serve them. It's beautiful to serve. So seva, for those who have chosen the Way of the Heart, it tends to be all of the time, not a part-time thing. This is one of the ways that I discovered what I called "manageable happiness" because in serving Heart, in serving others, there is a beauty, there is happiness, and there is a joy that arises.

Even if you don't become awakened, if you choose to serve Heart as a pathway towards awakening, you are choosing a path that can bring happiness because there's not much happiness in self-service. You can't say that selfishness or self-centeredness brings joy. But giving does. Being kind does. Being loving does. Taking care does.

So seva for me is a very important part of life. If we have to be here, how are we going to live this life?

The Way of the Heart is the Beauty Way. It's also the way to higher consciousness and the way to Enlightenment.

If we truly serve Heart, the main obstacle that's in the way of that service is the "I", the story of you. As you put the story of you aside, you're also putting the problems of you aside. Life is much more beautiful. It's up to you. Nobody's going to make you do anything you don't want to do. It took me ages to work out that seva was the best way to live life because it's not really something that we learn in the West. The West tends to be a bit selfish. It's more of an eastern way of living. The Way of the Heart is so beautiful and seva is the Way of the Heart in action.

Any questions, any statements, any challenges to this teaching today?

S: If you do seva because it's expected of you, would this stop you from acquiring good karma?

V: So the idea isn't to do seva to get good karma. The idea is to do service because it's a beautiful way to live. The Way of the Heart is a beautiful way to live. It's not about doing it because you want to get something. The whole idea of getting something, once again, heads us back into selfishness and self-obsession. True seva isn't about getting anything, it's about giving. It's about taking care. So the concern about karma: it is true if you become kind and loving and giving you do get good karma, but that's not why you do it. That's not why you do giving. You give for the sake of giving. You serve for the sake of serving. The Way of the Heart is not done to get something. The mind's affected in such a way that it just wants to take care and give.

~

S: You were talking about putting aside the story of you. How did you start to put aside the story of you?

V: I was working as a naturopath and psychotherapist and I had a clinic connected to my home. I just started to notice that every time I went to my clinic, as soon as I touched the handle on the door, the story of Vishrant disappeared, and when I walked through that door to a client who was waiting, I was there 100 per cent for the client. There was no Vishrant in the room. Vishrant had been left at the door.

After a while, I got to realise that that was a very peaceful way to live, without the story of Vishrant, without the troubles and the problems of Vishrant, so I started to extend that into other parts of my life – the way I was with my family, the way I was with my friends, the way I was with strangers. I started not to have the story of Vishrant. I started to be there in service to whoever I met and it was beautiful because I was loving people.

When there's no "I", there's no problem in loving, because there's no obstacle in the way anymore. So it began a long time ago when I recognised the beauty of not having a story of Vishrant.

~

S: Was it a specific practice that allowed you to be there 100 per cent for your clients when you started working or did you find that it happened automatically?

V: It was pretty automatic. I just gave my clients my totality, and if you're giving someone your totality, there's not much room for you in that totality. I was there 100 per cent for them. I was listening 100 per cent to them. I was watching 100 per cent, then I was diagnosing 100 per cent for them, treating 100 per cent for them. There wasn't any of me in the story and it was very beautiful. It was very automatic. It's just that the realisation – that this is a lovely space to live in – started to dawn on me, to just be here without a story. It's really nice because you enter the moment. Without a story, you can be in the moment. No past. No future. Just here. This is Zen.

~

S: It seems like you said silence is guiding you, but not Beingness guiding you. Aren't silence and the stillness distinct from Beingness? Doesn't seva help us experience silence but not Beingness?

V: There's a certain truth in that. I mean, if you want to find yourself as Truth, you turn awareness back to itself. You practise meditation. You practise openness. The thing about seva is it should be practised from a place of openness, and that openness will support Enlightenment because the mind's not contracting, it's not attracting awareness back to itself. We can go for Enlightenment through the practice of self-inquiry and meditation and we may even find something. But what do we do then? Do we sit in a chair all day and stare into space? Or do we actually do something?

My observation is if we move to doing something, that the way is the Way the Heart because you don't do it for yourself. You're doing it for others. You're in service. What do you do once you wake up? Or what do you do before you wake up and you're practising self-inquiry? You can't sit in a chair all day long. You choose a way of life that's beautiful, if you want, and I'm saying that the Way of the Heart is beautiful. It's a beautiful way to live this life. The observation that I have of the Way of the Heart in the marketplace is that of service or seva. That's how it shows itself. When you love people, when you love things, when you love this world, you deserve it. It's up to you.

~

S: How do you go about your life without a story?

V: Look, the story of you is not there all the time. You might think it is, but it's not. For example, you can ride a push bike and have someone riding next to you and be having an in-depth conversation with them, so who's riding the bike? You know, it's just automatic, it just happens, and this is how a lot of our life is lived. We're just here. We don't actually have a story of ourselves, and when we do have a story of ourselves, we're actually dreaming. If we're really present, there is no story of us. We're just here and the reason for that is because in truth, we are pure awareness. We're not this story. The story pretends to be us, but we are that that is aware of that. And we're here as that, all of the time. The story which is not us comes and goes.

~

S: Can you please talk about seva in terms of serving God?

V: Okay so you need a definition of God first. If you're going to talk about service of God, what is God? My understanding of God is that God is everything. Omnificent, everything, everyone – everything is God. So if you're serving God, you're serving everything, everyone. That's true service to God.

If the definition of God that I have is correct for you – that God is everything, from my perspective – service to everything is the Beauty Way. This is the Way of the Heart. I remember when I first started finding Truth itself, I'd sit all day long, just staring into space 18 hours a day. Then I realised that if you found this beauty, why not share it? Why not show it to other people? You've got to be here no matter what, so why not be in service? You can sit silently in bliss all day long or you can light people up and see if they can find the same space. See if they can find themselves as this because they are this. Everybody is pure awareness. A life of seva is a life of beauty.

~

S: Why is devotional service not a well-known concept in Western society?

V: Well, there are two paths to Enlightenment in India. There's the bhakti path and the yani path. The yani path, the path of discipline, and the bhakti path, the path of devotion which includes seva, includes the Way of the Heart. The combination of the yani path, the path of discipline, with the path of the Heart, the bhakti path, creates an environment for people to wake up in the marketplace. If we're just doing discipline, we can wake up in a monastery or an ashram or a cave. If we're just doing Heart, we may miss because we've not got the discipline to turn awareness back to itself or quieten the mind.

When we operate both of them together, the discipline and the Way of the Heart, we're setting ourselves up to create a mind that will support Enlightenment. People in the West don't really understand the bhakti path because the devotional path is not something that we do here. We do a little bit of the discipline and we get that. Most westerners actually like the yani path. They prefer discipline – whether it's through yoga or meditation or self-inquiry – but truthfully, if we want to wake up in the marketplace, we probably need both paths together.

The path of the Heart has us remove all of the obstacles that are in the way of love, and in removing these obstacles that are in the way of love we're creating a mind that will support Enlightenment. Self-inquiry and meditation can take you to Beingness, knowing self as Truth, and the Way the Heart can help produce a mind that will support that.

The bhakti path is a little bit different. The West doesn't really get into the devotional path very strongly. But all of those who have awakened are absolutely 100 per cent devoted to Truth. Otherwise, they would not be awake.

~

S: How do I know if my actions of service are truly for others, with nothing in it for me?
V: It took me a long time to learn to be altruistic because I was very clever at being seen as a giver by myself and by others. When I chose the Way of the Heart some 30 years ago, I wasn't good at it. I was good at being seen as being generous and loving and caring and all of the things you associate with the bhakti path or the Way the Heart, but the truth is, I was calculating it all, you know. I had to learn to give just for the sake of giving, and it took a lot of practice, but I had the intention of giving for the sake of giving, I wanted to be able to do that. I was sick of the selfish Vishrant. I had been around the block too many times. I wanted a different way of life and I knew that the Way of the Heart was that life, so I practised selfless giving. I practised altruism. I practised taking care. And I practised without looking for reward in it. It was a practice.

~

S: What do you think of Metta in general for people? What do you think about Metta in my case?

V: Yeah, Metta is the practice of giving out all of your love to the world. If you can open up enough to perceive love, if you're perceiving love, you become loving. You are giving your love to the world. If you're just doing Metta from the mind, you're probably just giving mind energy to the world. You have to be in touch with Heart. When you're in touch with Heart, when you're in touch with love, when you perceive it, you know you can't give it really because love is real and the one that wants to give it is not. The "I" is not real. But you can love. Love is here. And because love is here, you've become an oasis of it that others can then bathe in because you're perceiving love. You've opened your Heart and you've become a fountain of love. Just by being in the world with your Heart open is enough. Love does its own work. It loves.

~

S: Can being a mother or a parent count as devotional service?

V: Yes, it can. As a matter of fact, that's where a lot of people learn to become selfless because they have to put themselves aside or they have to learn to put themselves aside for the benefit of someone else. In the case of parents, their children. And in learning to put ourselves aside for the sake of someone else, we are learning the Way of the Heart, so yes.

~

S: I fear that by focusing on meditation and self-discovery, I will not be able to make a difference in the world. Are you in any way concerned with making a difference in the world?

V: Heck no. I teach the dharma. I teach a way to freedom. If people hear me, great. If people don't hear me, great. I have no expectation whatsoever. I'm like a lighthouse that turns around and around in the dark night shining its light to the ships. It has no expectation that the ships will see it. It has no expectation of what's going to happen. It just shines the light. That's pretty much the way it is. Just shine the light. No expectations.

~

S: If I help others because it makes me joyful, is that still a selfish motivation?

V: No, just keep helping others and be joyful. There's nothing wrong with joy. The world could do with a lot more joy actually. It's a pretty sad place for a lot of people. Bringing joy into the world is a gift in itself.

~

S: Sometimes I organise activities that will allow me to serve, but then I don't want to do them. How can I be more joyful whilst serving?

V: If you don't want to do them there's probably too much of you in the story. I just don't give myself a choice. You see, if we're total with that, if we give ourselves no choice, there's no story anymore. But if we start giving ourselves choices, we start going into story and we get caught in la la land. Be total in whatever you do. Give yourself no choice. No story. No story is best.

~

S: It seems I should spend a little more time around people and that's been a bit weird for me lately. I don't know if it's COVID-19. I don't think it's just COVID-19. They seem much more tense than they used to and contracted and talking faster and I don't seem to connect with them. I have to put effort into staying humble, really. I have friends who would listen to me talk about what satoris are like, which I think really would be great. I'm glad you suggested that. I'm not very motivated to do it, but I'm definitely going to do that. But if I'm going to inject some love into this, obviously, that's going to involve more than just me here with my wife. I don't know exactly what I'm asking. But I guess tips for dealing with people? You mentioned you stare at them. I do that sometimes if I go into satori. I did creep someone out that way.
V: Yeah. I've learned to look away because staring at people does freak them out.

Shame you're not here in Western Australia with me. We could go shopping together. I go to Coles to buy food for the sangha and I love going to Coles. Coles is a big shopping centre with wide aisles and bright lights and music and people, and I get to say hello to people and lift them energetically and have a bit of humour with them. It's just beautiful service. It's just a way of being in the world. I'm there for shopping, but I'm really there to say hello and lift.
S: Yeah, and now that I don't need them to feel good, it might even be better, purer, more kind.
V: Yeah. Look, people are so caught in their own stories. They're so caught in their dramas. For someone

to come and say hello to them can be a sweet thing, you know? And a smile, you know, maybe a joke?

You need to be a little bit careful where you are. I don't know where you are, but in Western Australia where I am currently [IN 2020], there is no COVID-19 so it's very easy to be here. Our boundaries, our borders are shut, so you don't see people with masks on that often because COVID-19 hasn't been here for a long time. I understand the rest of the world is having a real problem with infection and you have to be a little bit careful to protect yourself and to protect others.

~

S: When practising the Way of the Heart, are there still times when we need to be in seva to ourselves by taking time off and resting?

V: I just love it as a way of life and I have done for 30 years. I love being in service. I love taking care. I love loving. I don't need time off. Look, I have enough time alone. It's hard for me to answer this question because from my perspective, I just love people and I don't need space. I don't need personal space, not really.

I just love taking care of people, love lighting them up, love having a joke with them. Life is beautiful.

It's up to you. If you feel you need to take time out, take time out. The more you open up, the more you open your Heart, the more you remove the obstacles that are in the way, the more love is perceived.

The more you love people, the more you just want to be in service. It's up to you. It's very beautiful.

~

S: What would it look like to be in service inside of a relationship?

V: If you're in a relationship, you're lucky because you've got someone to love. When you love someone it's very beautiful and it doesn't really matter what they're like, because you're the one that's going to facilitate love or not, not them.

When we move into a relationship where we love the other and cherish the other, the relationship is very nourishing.

If we haven't got love in the relationship, and we're not cherishing the other, the relationship will be very dry, very dissatisfying. If we truly want to get the best out of our relationships, we need to cherish, we need to serve, we need to practise the Way of the Heart with our partners, with those who we want to love. Then the relationship becomes very beautiful, very nourishing, because love is very nourishing.

We may have to put a fair bit of our own belief systems aside to do that. We may have to put ourselves aside to be in true service to our partners. If all we want to do is be right all of the time, we're likely to destroy our relationships. Sometimes you have to put yourself aside to make it work. People might see that as co-dependence, but if you're doing it from a place of love, it's not co-dependence. It's only co-dependence if you're doing it because you don't want to be abandoned or rejected or something else like that.

There's this true beauty in being in service to your own partner as there is a true beauty in being in service to your children.

You get to experience love, and love is the true jewel of consciousness on this plane, nothing else.

Thank you for Satsang. Good to see you bravehearts here today.

CHAPTER SEVEN

What Is Your Core Message?

S: What is your core message?
V: I don't think I have a core message. Love is the only thing that has any value on this plane. And if you're willing to do what it takes to perceive love, I feel that you're on the right track. Every time we close, every time we contract, every time we defend ourselves, we cut ourselves off from love. And love is the most beautiful thing. It's just here.

So I don't think there's a core message of any kind, not really. Just a way of living life: the Way of the Heart, the Beauty Way.

From birth to adulthood, we've developed a heap of defences, a heap of ways of closing down, protecting ourselves from feeling, and all of these things that we've developed are now in the way of perceiving love. If you're willing to remove all of the obstacles, if you're willing to remove all of the things that close you and keep you defended, then love is always here. And it's very beautiful.

And when you perceive love, the way that that affects the mind, is you want to take care of everyone and everything. And that's very beautiful.

If there was more love on this planet, the planet would be a very different planet. Humanity would be very different. There wouldn't be any greed. There wouldn't be any wars or terrorism. Love builds bridges to everything and the mind tends to burn them.

So tune in, drop everything, and open up. Start to find the beauty inside of you. Start to find the treasure, the true treasure, the true jewel of consciousness: love. It's always here. If you do not perceive it, it's because somehow you're closed. Somehow, you're not open. Have a look and see what it is in you that's not open. What is it in you that's closed? Open up.

I say "openness counts for everything" because openness allows you to perceive love, allows you to heal the wounds of the heart, allows you to get out of the way enough for Enlightenment to occur. Openness counts for everything.

And it's up to you. We're talking about true rebellion. You start taking down your defences, you start removing the belief systems that contract you. You're rebelling against your own mind. You're rebelling against the programming that was put in there. This is the true value. It's up to you.

Are there any questions, any statements, any challenges to this teaching today?
S: Why is love the only thing that has value in this plane?
V: Well if you haven't realised that yet, you haven't really looked. Everything else the mind does is a form of suffering because the mind is programmed to desire things to be different than how they are. Now if we have a look at that, it's resistance to what is, and all forms of resistance to what is are suffering.

We're not really programmed to be happy. We're programmed to be unhappy in a lot of ways. And when we look at that, it's just a mind construct, something we create with the way we think, and the way we think is not even real because it's imagined. All thoughts are imagined.

Love is actually real and it's here. It's just that people put so many things in the way of it, they don't perceive it. It's always here. It's the true jewel of consciousness. It's so, so beautiful. Jesus said, "love thy neighbour". He didn't really say how. Open up, drop all of your defences, remove all of the belief systems that contract you, and there's love, it's here.

And that's up to you. Because you create your reality with the way you think. Nobody can do it for you. Only you.

~

S: How can I know if I'm truly open or just pretending and fooling myself?
V: It is very difficult because the mind has an amazing ability to fool itself, to lie to itself. It can create all sorts of imaginary things with its ability to imagine. Being able to discern the difference between what is real and what your mind is fabricating can be quite difficult. The one thing about what is real is it doesn't get stale. Anything the mind produces through imagination gets stale after a while. In looking for what is real and what is not real, staleness isn't a bad test.

Love is so fresh, so beautiful. Silence, true silence is lovely too. The mind's production of silence is not. You get stale.

It's difficult, because you're so used to listening to the mind. You're so used to believing it. Really, do you want to believe it? Why not doubt it a little bit and see what is really real. It's with doubt that we start to challenge the mind and all of the programming that was put into us by genetics and our parents, and our schooling and our government and whoever else, because we didn't program us. All of the programming was put in externally and it's worth having a look at and it's worth doubting. Anything that's not your own direct experience, put in a maybe column, take the power out of the belief.

~

S: Papaji once said that he hadn't met anyone ready for his final teaching. Do you have a final teaching and what would it be?

V: The final teaching is never said in words, it is in silence. The final teaching is actually the Buddha field that someone who is awake has, and if you are ready, if you have done the work to prepare the mind, just being in that Buddha field is enough for the transmission of the lamp to occur, for Enlightenment to happen. The final teaching is always the presence, in silence and stillness.

~

S: When you speak about love is that when one is out of the way and not just for others?

V: Yeah, it's not personal. Love is not personal. People think it's personal because the "I" claims it, but that's like something that's imagined claiming something that is real because the "I" is imagined. Take away your imagination and the "I" is not real. Love is real, but love's not personal, it's just here. A person can say, "Oh I love". Oh really? That's a bit of a false claim in a way because that which is imagined can't really claim that which is real. There's love, yeah, and maybe you feel like you love someone, but really what you are experiencing is love and love is not personal, it just is. And it's here, it's very beautiful, it's here. All you've got to do is get out of the way and discover it. It's here.

S: How do I tell the difference between feeling that I love and just love?

V: Feeling that I love and just love, does it really matter? Does it really matter? Why not just be okay with what is? If you're feeling love, be okay with that. The question would take you away from the experience of love because it puts you back in the mind. It's up to you. People get so complex. They want to understand. They want to know things. That's in the way as well.

The only thing a person needs to know to get free is surrender. Let go. You learn surrender by practising acceptance and let-go. That's the only thing that a human being needs to learn: unconditional surrender. If love's there, it's there. If it's not there, it's not there. Open up. Keep opening up, keep taking things away and keep whittling it away until there's nothing left, until there are no obstacles in the way.

And on the way through, witness the whole thing because as we witness things, they dissolve as well. It's only in unconsciousness that things continue. Stay aware. Stay aware of what your mind's doing. Witness it. Stay aware of everything. Witness it. This is the way.

S: I've heard you talk about one of your teachers whose only teaching was just "be happy". Does this work and do you teach this also?

V: No, I mean I understand that ... but you see, he doesn't say how to be happy, and the teacher was a Chinese physician that I had as an acupuncture teacher and he was a Taoist. To everything that happened, he would just say, "Be happy". It was very beautiful, but there was no indication as to how to be happy.

As long as there's an "I" in there, happiness is rather elusive because the "I" is constantly wanting things to be different, which is discontentment, not happiness. Or it's getting attached to something and fearful of losing it, which is not happiness, it's discontentment. The only way to be happy is for the "I" to diminish, and in practising openness, in practising taking down defences and belief systems, you're diminishing the "I". The happier you get, the less you are as an "I".

But that's up to you. It's not part of what most people do. Most people are looking to become bigger, better and more powerful which is personal growth. Spiritual growth is the opposite. It's about becoming less than. It's about diminishing the "I" until there's just nothing here. It's just all imagined anyway. But that's up to you. You've built the sandcastle, now take it down. It's going to fall down anyway. Everyone dies. Take it down before you die physically and wake up to your own true nature. Become free.

~

S: Does bantering and teasing encourage openness?
V: [LAUGHTER] No, but it definitely gives you an opportunity to practise surrender. You see, you look at life. Every time we contract or go into resistance or take offence or whatever, turn ourselves into a victim, we create a world of suffering for ourselves. But every time we contract, there is an opportunity to see what's contracting us and there's an opportunity to actually surrender. There's an opportunity to open up. There's an opportunity to remove the belief system that supports that contraction.

The people that tease us? The banter gives us opportunities, like devices that show us where we're stuck. Rather than avoiding it, use it as a teaching to show you what's happening inside of you. It's all good. The whole world can be your teacher if you let it. Every time you contract, there's a place there that you're unconscious in. Become conscious. Have a look. What's contracting you? Open up. What belief systems are contracting you? What expectations weren't met? Undo those belief systems. Become free. You create your reality and you can undo it. You can.

~

S: Gautama the Buddha is said to have taught that when true love is present, it will be there even for someone who is sawing off your limbs. It seems like an extreme example, but do you think this is possible?
V: It's not only possible, it's absolutely true. If you're open, love is there. It's not personal, it's there and it affects the mind in such a way that the mind feels

that it loves even the one that might be hurting it. The only thing that stops us from perceiving love really is closure, when we contract, when we go into resistance, when we get defensive. Have a look and see for yourself. I don't know ... I've never experienced anyone cutting off my arms so I can't really answer the question with agreement or disagreement in a way, but I know that when love is there, even the people who're trying to hurt you, you love. Even when things are going wrong, you love, if you're open enough, if you're undefended enough.

~

S: Is only feeling with no accompanying change in belief healing?

V: No, not really because if we don't change the way we think we're going to recreate the wounding, even if we do feel it and heal it. That's the problem. Healing has two aspects to it. One is the willingness to meet whatever pain is inside us, whatever wounding is inside us. That willingness is a requirement. And there's also a requirement that we don't reproduce the same wounding with the way we think. Unless the belief systems that were involved in creating the wounding in the first place – which are always victim-orientated – aren't challenged and undone, we're likely to recreate whatever wounding has been there, even if we have healed it by feeling it.

~

S: I've been practising meditation and self-inquiring with the hope of waking up for years, but I'm not yet enlightened. What might I be doing wrong?

V: My question to you would be: are you actually hanging out with someone who's awake or are you trying to do it by yourself? Someone who's awake is going to help you wake up. Trying to do it by yourself is pretty difficult. The ego is an amazing survival mechanism. It's a million years old and it's brilliant at it. Someone who's already awake, who's been through it, knows how it survives and will help you get through, first of all, by providing a Buddha field that you can actually expand your mind in and disappear in. Second, they know all the traps. If you really want to wake up, find someone who's awake and hang out with them.

~

S: Why did you choose to teach a Buddhist path to Enlightenment?

V: My teacher Osho Rajneesh spoke so kindly and so beautifully about Gautama the Buddha, I fell in love with him. I fell in love with his teachings. I also started to recognise clearly that his sutras, what he was teaching, was true. After satoris began, it became very obvious that what the Buddha was teaching was absolutely right. It was just a vehicle or a methodology towards higher consciousness that had worked for 2500 years. Why should I create a new one when there's one already there, a great vehicle, that's already there?

The only side of Buddhism that I thought could be a little different is instead of being life negative, being life positive. In other words, celebrating life, instead of denying life. Enjoying it, celebrating it – which is another thing I picked up from Osho Rajneesh. They say that Buddhism in some degrees is bitter, and Taoism in some degrees is sweet. Well, I like the sweet. I think life should be celebrated. We have this amazing opportunity to be here. We have this vehicle, this spacesuit to dance with. Why not dance? Why not play? Why not squeeze the juice out of life? Why not find ourselves as Truth? The only thing that needs to be denied or renounced is this, nothing else.

~

S: In Buddhism, they talk about some people not being able to wake up in this lifetime. Do you think anybody can wake up?

V: I don't know. See, what comes into play here is karma. Some people call it grace and now we're heading into the unknown. I just don't know. When someone says "by grace", from my perspective, all they're saying is well, I don't really know.

But people want to know. They want to know because they want to control, they want to manipulate, so they want to know. The only thing you need to know is how to surrender unconditionally. That's all you need to know.

~

S: Why does time pass quickly if there's less mind, yet slowly when we think?

V: Well, time is mind-made. There is only now. This is it. There is only now. Time is a product of thinking. There is only now. This is the only time that is real. There is no past. There is no future. There is only now. This is real. If we were locked in a darkened room, a black room, how do we know what time it is? It's just a mind thing. It's a mind construct.

There's only now. It's always now. It's quite nice now. The more you move into the moment and being aware of what is real in the moment – nothing you think is real, by the way – the less time that you perceive. The less you perceive this middle understanding of time, the more present you are, there is no time, there is only now. It's very beautiful.

~

S: What does it mean to go beyond the mind?
V: Okay. To go beyond the mind, to go beyond psychology, well, the good news is we're not the mind, but most people think they are the mind and the body. But that's just not true. There's something that is aware of the mind – something that is aware that is here always. That is beyond the mind.

When that discovers itself, when awareness turns on itself and stays on itself, then that is Enlightenment. Instead of living as a mind and a body as an "I", there's existing as Beingness, our own true nature. Beyond the mind is what we really are. The mind is fraudulent. It claims to be us, but it is not. Find that that is aware of the mind. Find that that is pure consciousness and you've found your true self.

~

S: How do I not lose myself in psychology while trying to undo the mind?
V: It's pretty difficult because you've been trained to problem solve at school, 12 years of it or thereabouts. Most human adults are problem solvers and

psychology is all about problem solving in a lot of ways. What works is witnessing the mind. You just watch it. Just watch the mind. Develop the silent witness that watches, because when you become aware of things, they dissolve. So just witness. Just watch. If you're going to do psychology on yourself, you're basically going into another dream. You're lost in another dream. You don't get out of dreams by dreaming. Start witnessing the mind. That works.

~

S: Why do you say that meditation is the answer to every question?

V: Because every question is nonsense and meditation takes you to silence and stillness which is beautiful and real. The question "Who am I?" is the only real question. Who am I? Or what am I? Or who's aware? This is a good question, the answer to which cannot be put by the mind, can only be known through the direct experience of that which is aware of the mind becoming aware of itself. That is a really good question. Who am I really? Discount the idea that you're a mind, that you're an "I", or that you're a body, and find out who you really are.

~

S: Sometimes, I forget that you are Beingness and I project that you're like me, an ego-based person. Did you ever do this with your teachers? And how can I stop projecting onto you?

V: Of course I did because that's what the ego does. It projects its understandings onto everything, and understands things from its limited knowledge.

The only way that you can really get to understand someone who's awake is to wake up because all of the reference points that you understand your life with as an ego aren't there anymore. The ego thinks it's been somewhere and it thinks it's going somewhere. Beingness is just here. It doesn't have a past or a future because that's just rubbish. That's another dream. Ego-based reality and being-based reality are quantumly different. There's no connection. One is real, one is not. Asking the question, "Who is aware?" or "What is aware" and following the "I" back to its source can show your true nature. Then the "I" is shown up as absolutely false. You were never an "I". You never could have been. It was an imagined character that you put together with your imagination. You are pure Beingness. You are pure awareness. Without a thought, you are. Before thought begins, you are.

~

S: When you let everything go and dedicated yourself to Being, did you cast off all worldly belongings?
V: I gave my life away. I was prepared to die. Whatever it took, I was willing to do. I gave my life to Truth and another way of saying that is I gave my life to God. "Thy will be done, not my will" any longer. See people, they want to wake up, but then they want to have something after awakening. That's not how it works. The ego surrenders unconditionally. No conditions. You're putting yourself in the hands of something from the perspective of the "I", of something that could kill you. You don't know. You don't know if you'll ever have anything ever again. You don't know.

You've given it all away. It's not that I physically gave anything away really, but I gave my life to Truth and everything got lost anyway. It really left anyway.

The whole idea of being attached to things is just prison. There's so much freedom in unconditional surrender, but it's frightening. So people don't get involved in it. They're frightened of losing control. They're frightened of losing this or that. And the deal is really simple: everything for Truth and nothing for you as an "I". Everything for God and nothing for you as an "I" – and it's the best deal in town.

~

S: You were speaking of discounting the idea that I'm a body and a mind. What's the best way to do this?
V: Oh, you can't discount the idea that you're a body and a mind, not really, and be successful at it. You can let it go temporarily, but it'll come back. If you really want to be free, you have to have awareness discover itself. You have to wake up. There is no other way to be free. The ego resurrects itself over and over again until awareness is aware of itself. Then it just can't because it's obviously not real. If you really want to get rid of the "I", wake up. Turn awareness onto itself, remove all of the obstacles that are in the way of that. That's best. The idea of the mind discounting itself and discounting the body is just another dream. It's not real.

~

S: I know somewhere within that you're awakened, but it still makes me uncomfortable. When you psychologically provoke people in your Satsangs it seems mean. How do I separate from this discomfort and just witness?

V: What are you willing to pay for freedom? What price are you willing to pay to be free? Every time you contract, you put yourself in prison and that prison is where you suffer. Every time you disagree with life, every time you resist, you suffer, but that's your doing.

From time to time, I set up devices so people can practise surrender, practise acceptance. Because really, it's the only thing we need to learn. We learn unconditional surrender by practising acceptance which is a spiritual practice.

Everything you've got is going to get taken off you anyway. Why not do it sooner than later? Why not give up now? The Bodhi tree that Buddha sat under didn't mind whether he woke up or not, but the Buddha woke up because he surrendered unconditionally. He didn't do anything, he just surrendered unconditionally, which is a non-doing, the hardest thing for us to learn.

We learn it through the practice of acceptance, and how can we practise acceptance unless things aren't going our way?

~

S: I've heard teachers say to call off the search. What is your understanding of this statement?

V: Well, it's very simple. When you're in the presence of someone who's awake, you call off the search because if you stop seeking at that point you may find yourself as Truth in the Buddha field. But you don't call off the search while you're looking by yourself. As a matter of fact, it is the search and the thirst for truth that gives you the opportunity to come home. But when you're in the presence of someone who's awake, you let go of everything. You let go of the search as well. And in that letting go, Enlightenment can occur.

Until then, if you're by yourself, every endeavour, everything needs to be put into finding yourself as Truth. If you call it off and you're still ego-based, you will remain ego-based if you're not in the presence of someone who's awake. The presence of someone who's awake is like a doorway into your own true nature. It's the gift of Satsang.

~

S: You speak of meditation, self-inquiry, and the game of zero as practices. What is the most important practice a seeker should commit to in the pursuit of higher consciousness?

V: The practice of openness, because it takes away everything, prepares the mind for Enlightenment, allows you to perceive Heart, and allows you to heal the wounds of the Heart. The practice of openness from my perspective is the most important spiritual practice you can have and it's the practice that most people don't do. They practise resistance, they practise trying to know, trying to control. What about practising let-go? What about practising openness? What about supporting the Heart?

Up to you. You create your reality with the way you think. You're either going to practise openness or you're not. Up to you.

~

S: How can the path of love lead to knowing oneself as Truth?

V: Well, if you're perceiving love, that means you're wide open, which means the obstacles that are in the way of Enlightenment are not there. Check it now. The way to live this life is to wear your heart on your sleeve and to always be vulnerable, to always be open. A mind that can do this is a mind that has prepared itself for Enlightenment. It's a mind that stays equanimous.

~

S: I feel dense around a potential housemate candidate. Should I keep where I live a sanctuary or should I practise being open to this density?

V: Have a look yourself. What supports higher consciousness and what doesn't? Always be involved in what supports higher consciousness and try to avoid what creates lower consciousness.

The only way out of this Samsara life of basically suffering is Enlightenment and higher consciousness supports that.

So whatever supports higher consciousness, whatever supports your clarity, whatever supports you in getting free, support that. I don't teach people generally speaking who are in monasteries or ashrams who have sanctuary. I teach lay people. I teach people who have families, people who have a job that they have to keep, people who are in the marketplace. But we still need sanctuary, because without sanctuary, we don't have the clarity to see what's in our way.

We don't have the clarity to remove the obstacles that are in the way. Sanctuary is important. Always support higher consciousness, always.

~

S: What did you do to fuel your thirst for Truth? Is this something that you were born with, or something that was developed?

V: There's a good chance I was born with it. I've always been interested in the meaning of life, the purpose of life as far back as I can remember. I haven't found any meaning of life yet or any purpose to life. It's just life. It just is.

We want to find purpose. We want to find meaning because the ego wants to feel secure. I can't find a purpose or a reason. There's just life. Our need to know makes us feel secure if we think we know, but the truth is we don't know and it's okay to not know.

In Buddhism, they talk about having a beginner's mind and a beginner's mind is someone who doesn't know. And because they don't know, existence can show them. The moment we think we know, we're actually lost, we've closed ourselves off. So the truth is, we're living in not knowing all of the time, but we try to know so we feel safe. There's nothing safe. Everything really is unknown. And unknown is okay.

~

S: How do I develop a beginner's mind?

V: Well, you had one when you were a kid and then you got taught that you had to know things so you could pass exams and get ahead in school. You found out that knowing made you feel safe, feel secure. To develop a beginner's mind, you actually have to realise that you don't know, because we don't. You start finding Beingness itself, you start having satoris, and it's really obvious you don't know because even what you find can't be described, not really.

As long as we think we know, we're lost, we're stuck. We've closed ourselves off.

Just try. Practise not knowing. I don't know. I don't know. And you'll find you're actually finally being honest, because we don't.

~

S: How would I know if the teachings of a spiritual teacher are authentic?
V: Does it make any difference if they work? A false teacher can give good teachings just as well as a true teacher. But what's a true teacher? A true teacher is someone who's awake. A true teacher is someone who's speaking from their own direct experience in the moment.

But even if the teacher's not true, even if the teacher isn't awake, the teaching might be good. If they're teaching surrender, or they're teaching acceptance, if they're teaching the Way of the Heart, if they're teaching openness, great. They're teaching self-inquiry, great, teaching meditation, great, teaching yoga, great, and Tai Chi, great. Doesn't really matter. It's up to you. Put your totality into whatever you're doing. That works.

~

S: I found books, dharma talks, and ancient texts helpful, but feel my greatest and hardest teachings in life

will be from learning by direct contact with my masters. From your experience, would you agree with this?
V: I think like everybody else I began by collecting knowledge thinking that somehow that would raise my consciousness levels towards Enlightenment. That's an absolute fallacy. No amount of knowledge learned from books set anyone free. No amount of knowledge from books ever healed a wound of the Heart. No amount of knowledge from books ever showed someone Heart.

There's a fallacy there. We were brought up to believe that if we studied books and were able to repeat answers, we'd get somewhere, but in higher consciousness, that's just not true. You really want to know? You actually have to practise something that shows you. Meditation, self-inquiry, the practice of openness, these things work. The practice of witnessing the mind, this works. But these are practices, these aren't knowledge. Knowledge is the booby prize. You really want to find out, practise something that works.

~

S: How can I give up the desires of what I want and just be happy?
V: Well, you probably can't just be happy. You see, the desire to be happy is dissatisfaction itself. That's you making yourself unhappy by desiring happiness. Find that that doesn't have desires. Find that that is just aware. Find that.

You can't be happy inside the mind. It's not programmed for it. You have to go beyond the mind. Find that that's aware of the mind. That's best.

~

S: I've heard that a person should seek a master who has an absence of craving, aversion and delusion. Do you think these are the qualities I should look for in a teacher?

V: If you come to someone who's claiming to be awake, and your mind starts disappearing, and you find that there's nothing but emptiness, you're in the right place.

~

S: Is it true that a teacher points us towards a new way of being in the world?

V: Oh, it can do. A teacher can point you to a new way of being. But the problem is you don't make it. The question is, is it true that a teacher points us to a new way of being in the world? Yeah, but you don't make it. If you were talking about Enlightenment, you as an "I" don't make it. You don't get to that party because you're false, you're not real. What's real is that that's aware of the "I" and that's who you are, and that's always there.

So it's not like suddenly you're at your final destination because you've been looking for it. No, you're already at your final destination, you're just not aware of it, that's all. Your awareness is on the mind and on the "I" instead of on itself. Turn awareness onto itself, find yourself, and then the "I" disappears. Because the "I" is just a figment of your imagination based on reference points from the past projected to the future and a few belief systems – all imagined, none of it real, not one bit. You are pure Beingness and you are here now.

~

S: Is it important to resonate with a teacher's message in order to understand it?

V: The only thing that's important is to learn surrender, nothing else. If you can learn surrender, you've learnt what you need to know. Whether you resonate with someone who's awake or you don't resonate with someone who's awake is irrelevant. Surrender is what counts.

If someone's awake, they have a Buddha field. In that Buddha field you can find yourself as Truth. That's all you need to know. Die in that Buddha field. Find yourself as Truth. It's not personal. It's never personal. The idea of personal is just a fallacy in itself because the "I" is not real. Who you are is before the "I". Who you are is vast everythingness, vast nothingness. Find that, find that that's aware and find this to be so.

There is nothing else to do here. Get free. Do everything that you possibly can to get free. This requires a revolution against the way you've been programmed. Your mind is the only obstacle in the way of you knowing yourself as Truth. The way it's been programmed is probably going to keep you trapped. Watch the mind, witness it, undo it, surrender it. Accept life as it is and become free. This is up to you. Nobody can do that for you. Your willingness is what will take you. Your unwillingness will keep you stuck in lower consciousness. Your choice. You're creating your reality with the way you think. Remove all obstacles in the way of freedom, all the belief systems that create contraction in you. Undo everything until there's nothing left in the way and then you've done whatever you can to support Enlightenment. That's all you can do. It will either happen or it will not happen. It is by grace. Anybody who thinks they know or says they know does not know. We create our own reality by the way we think. Who's aware of the thinker? What's aware of the thinker? This is interesting.

Thank you for Satsang, good to see you bravehearts here today.

CHAPTER EIGHT

Suffering and Addictions

V: All human beings have an addictive nature. It's just part of being human. We get addicted to that which changes our consciousness or makes us feel better or takes us away from discomfort. We get addicted to just about anything from drugs, to alcohol, to food, to working, to gaming, to gambling, to our mobile phones, to social media – you name it. Anything that can change our consciousness has the potential for us to become addicted to it.

And in itself, it usually is an avoidance of something. It makes us feel comfortable. It takes us away from something that's not comfortable. So after work, people have a drink "to take the edge off", they say. Well really, they're just trying to change their consciousness. They're medicating themselves. And the same goes with drugs, medicating themselves. Some people medicate themselves with food. Some people medicate themselves by becoming do-aholics, and that's a pretty good one. They don't usually see it as an addiction. But they get addicted to constantly doing, because it looks productive and it takes them away from feeling something they don't want.

So a lot of our addictions are just escape mechanisms or medication to medicate us away from something we don't want to feel, possibly towards something we do want to feel. The problem with that is if you're into higher consciousness, you've got to stop running away. You've got to stop avoiding. You've got to allow yourself to be with what is, because as long as you're avoiding, as long as you're medicating yourself in some way, you're probably keeping yourself in lower consciousness.

It's in stillness and silence that we see the mechanisms of what's happening around us and what's happening in our minds. As long as we're using escape methodologies, we're likely to miss what's happening, particularly if they're drugs and alcohol, because they don't raise our consciousness levels, they lower our consciousness levels. Talking about this particular subject will probably upset a few people because people like their medication. They like their escape mechanisms. They think, "Oh that makes me feel comfortable?" Well sure, it actually does, but if you're into higher consciousness, it's in the way. It's another obstacle. It's another obstacle that keeps you locked in lower consciousness.

So to avoid suffering, people medicate themselves. But there's another way to avoid suffering: stop resisting life. That works. Stop contracting against life, stop resisting and learn to become accepting of life as it is. In that acceptance, life becomes quite lovely. In our non-acceptance of life, well, it's pretty awful, and hence our need or our perceived need to medicate ourselves with something that's probably addictive.

If you want to heal the wounds of your Heart, you have to stop running away. You have to be willing to feel what's there. If you're interested in raising your consciousness levels, you've got to stop running away. You've got to learn how to rest and be relaxed without taking something that's going to change your consciousness levels.

If you want to become enlightened, you have to surrender unconditionally. And there's no running away in that. But it's always up to you. You're the one creating your reality. No one else is doing it to you. What do you really want, and what are you willing to pay for it?

Addictions eventually tend to be damaging. They tend to ruin relationships and ruin jobs, ruin families, ruin long lives, ruin your health. Because as the addiction goes on, we need more and more and more of whatever it is to make us feel better or to take us away from whatever we're avoiding. It's good to sit down and actually have a good look at what you're actually doing. Are you running away? Are you avoiding? What are you actually up to with whatever you're using to change your consciousness levels?

Whatever addiction you're playing with to avoid your pain, have a look. It's up to you. This is your life.

Are there any questions, any statements or any challenges to this teaching today?

S: I've noticed I'm addicted to dream. I constantly fall into dreaming of a perfect future. Why is this so addictive?

V: Because it takes you away from the imperfect now, because you're not seeing life is perfect as it is, so you're looking for something better, something later.

You've got a hope that things are going to be better later. And of course, the other side of that particular coin is the fear that they're not. And so hope always comes with fear. But both of them are projections to the future. They're not real. Now is real. Our projections to the future aren't. But those projections have the potential to take us away from feeling what's here now, which may be anything. Could be despair, it could be pain, could be anything. And so some people sell hope, the hope of later. It's an opiate that takes you away from what's here now. And it's not real. There's nothing real about the future, there's only now. Now is real. Only now. So avoid hope. Avoid hope, be here now, be with what is now, be accepting of what's here now, and be free. Or you're going to start living in a projection of the future – which is what hope is – and it's not real. You're not even living in reality anymore. You're living in la-la land, and in your head, in a projection. Have a look and see.

~

S: Do you mean physical or mental pain?
V: Okay, both physical and mental pain can be experienced with or without resistance. Mental pain tends to be resistance if you have a look at it, but not necessarily. So you have a look at pain. You can have pain, and then watch what happens. If you're not in resistance to it, you're not actually suffering. The moment you move to resistance in any way, shape or form, you've begun the suffering, and the more resistance you put towards that pain, the more intense the suffering is. And so in that way, we actually have or can have con-

trol over how much suffering we have. Because if we're not willing to put in the resistance, if we're willing to accept it as it is, there's a hell of a lot less suffering.

~

S: Can meditation be used to help a seeker overcome an addictive nature to either coffee, social media, food, alcohol, excessive exercise or working?

V: Ah, the best way to overcome an addiction is to stop the addiction.

That might sound simplistic, but that's the true answer. And when a person is willing to stop, they will stop. If they're not willing to stop, nothing can help them. No amount of anything can help them, whether it's meditation or anything else. When you want to stop, you put the effort into stopping, you'll stop. Otherwise, you won't stop. This is the thing with people who are addicted: if they're willing to stop, and they put the effort into stopping, they'll stop. Nothing else will stop them. If they're not willing, no way is it gonna stop. Willingness is what makes a difference.

Meditation allows you to quieten your mind, allows you to see through the mind, so it will probably allow you to see what you're actually up to, what the addiction you're involved in is doing, and give you a better understanding of the complexities of that addiction: the good, the bad and the ugly of it. But even if you see it all and you see how detrimental that addiction is to you, if you're not willing to stop, you ain't gonna stop. That's not going to happen. It's only the willingness to stop and the willingness to make that happen that works.

~

S: Did you ever have any addictions? And if so, how did you overcome them?

V: Heck, yeah, I had every addiction. I grew up in a family where my grandparents had a couple of bottles of beer every night before they went to bed while watching television and I just thought that was normal. My dad had a drink every night. My mom had a drink every night. That was normal. All of my relatives were big drinkers. It was normal. I grew up with addiction. I grew up with the gambling addiction as well. My father was very much into the horses and the greyhounds and anything, anything that you could bet on. So I grew up with some major addictions in my life and just in my family. I just thought it was normal. I didn't know that it was wrong or bad or unhealthy at that stage as a kid, I just thought it was normal.

So needless to say, I took up exactly the same addictions, because kids copy their parents. And it wasn't until a lot of years later that I realised this is not serving me, this is not serving anybody, and these addictions do not help me heal the wounds of my Heart. These addictions destroy the relationships that I've got. They don't help build bridges, they help burn them. So I had a good look at these addictions. I think I gave up gambling when I was about 20-21, completely, because it was clear to me, if you gamble and you win, someone else loses. That's not fun. That's not the way. That's not beautiful.

As far as alcohol is concerned, well, I kept that one going for a while, and just got to see how destructive it was, what a fool you make of yourself when you've drunk too much, how it actually destroys your ability to think properly. And yeah, it lubricates things, it makes things easier, but the cost is too high. And so I think I was 24 when I started a magazine called Addicts because I was a publisher back then, and this magazine went out to all the rehabilitation centres and all the doctors' surgeries in Western Australia. I produced this periodical – I think it went out monthly – and it was full of the different types of addictions and the different treatments you could get from where and when and what, and at the time I was still smoking cigarettes as well. Of course, I'm reading all of these articles about how cigarettes cause cancer, and I'm publishing the magazine, and I started to feel a bit like a hypocrite because I had thought addictions were just about drugs, but it's about a lot of things. It's about a lot of things. So I got a clear understanding of addiction because I was writing editorials on it each month, and how it affected people, how it destroyed their families, and how it was an escape methodology.

That set me up for an interest in addictions. And so I think a few years later, some 10 years later, I trained with the Drug and Alcohol Authority in Western Australia as an addictions counsellor because I was interested in it. At some point, I felt like a hypocrite because I hadn't tried some of the things that I was actually talking to people about so I tried everything once or twice and I saw clearly that all of those things are very addictive. All of the drugs are very addictive.

Alcohol is very addictive. Gambling is very addictive. Food is very addictive. All of these things are simply escape mechanisms to take us away from discomfort, usually in the beginning, at least. As I was more interested in healing the wounds of my Heart than running away from them, the addictions were ceased. I decided to allow myself to be with what is rather than find ways to escape through medication and whatever else.

But the world that I'd entered – the world of addicts, because I was treating them – showed me the level of suffering that addictions cause, how they destroy families, how they destroy human beings. There's no upside to being an addict, only a downside. You end up becoming a massive liar because you lie to make it work for yourself to get your product, to get whatever you're addicted to. You become unreliable, you become flaky, you become untrustworthy and you wreck your health. You wreck your relationships. Not a good idea, a bad idea. The problem with giving up addictions is you have to face the music of what's inside of you. And it's going to probably be pretty unpleasant if you've been an addict for a while, and you've done a fair bit of damage. But that's the price. That's the price you have to pay. You have to be willing to feel, and in the willingness to feel our wounding, we heal our wounding. Up to you. You're gonna create your reality.

~

S: Is it possible to be addicted to the Buddha field of an awakened being? And is there a risk of becoming too dependent on the teacher?

V: The addiction to the Buddha field is an addiction to your own true nature. A Buddha field is produced by awareness being aware of itself in a human being. If you become addicted to that, you're becoming addicted to the energy field of Beingness – and as a result of that addiction, you'll probably do anything you can to find that in yourself. That encourages a thirst for freedom, the thirst for Enlightenment. That is not a bad addiction. I recall clearly that I had that addiction. I was absolutely categorically addicted to the Buddha field of my teachers. I would tune into them anytime I could and I'd be with my teachers anytime I could because of that Buddha field. And what happened as a result of my mind's love affair with that Buddha field is that Buddha field started finding me. Truth started finding me. I started finding that space when my teachers weren't around, when I wasn't in Satsang.

So tune in. As far as becoming addicted or dependent on a teacher, if you're lost in the jungle, and you've got a guide who is taking you out, and you do not know the way out, you are dependent on that guide. And the same goes for Enlightenment. It's really difficult to wake up by yourself. The ego is a survival mechanism. It will do anything to survive. If you're with someone who's awake, they'll help you out of that jungle too. It's up to you. I had teachers the whole way through. I had Osho Rajneesh for eight years until he died. And then the Advaita Vedanta people came and I had them. And I followed their instruction to the letter. I didn't arrogantly think that somehow I knew better. How can you know better than somebody who's further ahead than you? If you follow the instructions of those who are awake, you'll get free. And if you really look at those instructions, you'll discover that they're not original anyway. They've been taught for 10,000 years or more. But if you follow them, you have a chance. If you decide to do it your way, you'll probably miss the boat. It's your choice.

To be with someone who's awake is a gift. To be able to have access to someone who's awake is access to the door into your own consciousness, access to freedom. It's brilliant. It's up to you though. You sit in the presence of someone who's awake, your mind will expand and start to disappear, and this puts you in exactly the right place for knowing yourself as Truth. It's up to you though. You're the one who's going to put yourself there or not. You're the one who's going to be attracted or not. I was very attracted to the awakened ones. I could feel their field of energy. I could feel it so strongly that if they came to Perth, and they landed at the airport, I could feel them landing. Because it's a frequency. You can tune into it. My mind would start expanding. It would start disappearing. And in that space, we start to have the benefit of awareness turning onto itself and discovering itself. It's up to you. How thirsty are you for Truth? How thirsty are you to wake up?

I think the greatest mistake seekers make is they think that just sitting in the Buddha field is enough. No. Sitting in the Buddha field creates the right ground, but if you're not prepared to do what it takes, if you're not prepared to prepare the mind for Enlightenment, well it's probably not going to happen. Openness counts for everything. Take down your defence systems. Become present to reality through meditation. Self-inquire. These things work.

Thank you for that Satsang. Good to see you bravehearts here today.

CHAPTER NINE

Accessing Superconsciousness

S: Can you please talk about accessing superconsciousness?
V: Okay, so superconsciousness is awareness knowing self as Truth. When awareness is aware of itself, when consciousness is aware of itself, if that's in an ongoing way, that is Enlightenment. Accessing it, to have a glimpse or a satori, can be achieved in a number of different ways, self-inquiry being one of the best. Being in the presence of somebody who's awake being one of the best. But it can happen at any time. A person can have a satori or a glimpse of their true nature at any time – walking on a beach, washing dishes, meditating.

Self-inquiry, asking the question, "Who's aware?" or "Who am I?" is the mind directly trying to access Beingness, directly trying to turn that that's aware back to itself. And that's an effective methodology. So accessing Beingness isn't that difficult if you're diligent with your practice of self-inquiry or meditation.

For awareness to stay on awareness or consciousness to stay aware of itself continuously requires a mind that will be equanimous, a mind that is not creating disturbance, not attracting attention back to itself. So that's actually the difficult bit. It's relatively easy to get a glimpse of who we truly are. People can even do it by taking certain drugs, but it doesn't really mean anything unless it can stay, unless awareness can stay aware of itself, unless Enlightenment actually occurs.

That's a little more difficult because the mind has to support that, and every time the mind contracts or goes into resistance against the world as it is, it creates a problem – it creates a contraction, a resistance that awareness goes back to. People can have awakening where they turn awareness onto itself and then the mind contracts for some reason and awareness goes back to the mind. Then there's a sense, at least from the mind's perspective, that something is lost. Of course, Beingness can never be lost, it is always here. People think that Beingness might be somewhere else, but it's not, it's always here,

Everybody is actually at their final destination right now. But the mind likes to think there's a bit of a journey. It likes to think there's some way to go or something to get. All that needs to occur is for awareness to become aware of itself and stay aware of itself. That's all. It's here now, it's not somewhere else. It's not in another lifetime. It's here now. So we tend to live or make our home where our Heart is and those who fall in love with Truth, with Beingness, that is where their Heart is. And that is where their home is. So you could say that there is a love affair between Beingness and the mind, and in this love affair, the mind lays itself down. In unconditional surrender, Enlightenment occurs.

So accessing higher consciousness isn't so difficult. Removing all of the things that can attract the mind constantly when it goes into resistance to the world, that's difficult because a lot of those contractions, a lot of that resistance is the result of belief systems that have never been truly examined, that were probably put in by other people, or society or religion. When the expectations on these belief systems aren't met, quite often a contraction or resistance occurs. In undoing the mind, in taking away these belief systems or discrediting them, they lose their power. And so does the amount of contraction and resistance. And so the work, if there is any work to do, is just undoing the mind, preparing the mind for superconsciousness or Enlightenment. Beingness doesn't need any work done, it is perfect as it is, and it's already here. It's just the mind needs to be able to support it. And so a mind that actually has undone itself is ready. And then all that person really needs to do is either self-inquire, meditate, or be in the presence of somebody who is already awake and awakening can occur.

Up to you, this is your life.

S: What's the most effective or efficient way of doing the work to prepare the mind for superconsciousness?
V: Yeah, look, we are all in relationship in one way or another whether it's with a partner or whether it's with business colleagues, whether it's with friends or children, or just the people we meet day to day. We're always in relationships, and in these relationships, our contractions and our resistances to life show up because we don't agree with what's going on necessarily.

The stronger we disagree, the more we are against what is, the more chance we are going to contract, the more chance we are going to take ourselves into lower consciousness. Our best teachers are probably the people that we don't get along with because they are going to show us where we contract and where we resist. They begin to show us our belief systems that keep us in contraction, so as a seeker, it's not a bad idea to value these people who you don't get along with because they can be your best teachers.
S: Can we disagree and not contract?
V: Oh, heck yeah. You can disagree and not contract. You can see something completely wrong that's happening in the world and not contract. It's not that you agree with it, you're just not into contracting. You're not into going into resistance, because you're conscious enough not to, because you've practised, and you've undone belief systems to some degree that create those contractions.

Any time we put doubt into a belief system it loses its power. But if we believe that belief system to be absolutely true, it is powerful. Have a look and see. We can be okay with the way the world is even when we don't agree with it. We can remain open. We don't have to close. We don't have to resist. And what's more, our closure and our resistance doesn't make any difference, doesn't change anything. Actually, it just hurts us because resistance is suffering. We create that suffering for ourselves through our resistance which changes nothing. Have a look and see for yourself.

~

S: How do you recognise someone who has super-consciousness?

V: There's only one way that I know that is foolproof because anybody can say the right words, have the right mannerisms and put themselves in a position of claim by saying I am enlightened or I'm this or that. Anybody can do that, but one thing that people who aren't awake can't do is produce a Buddha field – a field of energy that can be perceived that quietens the mind and expands it. Someone who's awake carries that Buddha field, always. If it's not there, sometimes it means they are not fully awake yet. But someone who is fully awake always has a Buddha field around them and this Buddha field is beautiful. This is the only way that I know that you can tell if someone's awake or not. What field of energy do they actually carry? When awareness is aware of itself, or consciousness is aware of itself, a Buddha field is produced, a field of energy that is very beautiful, that expands the mind and quietens it.

~

S: Resistance does not change anything. Wouldn't it cause emotional disturbance, which influences choices, which influences behaviour?

V: Oh, yes, it does. It influences your behaviour, there's no doubt about that. I'm saying that your resistance, which is suffering, doesn't change anything in the world, really. It might change how you operate, but it doesn't change anything in the world. Not really.

Your suffering doesn't change the world. You can move to change things in the world from a place of non-suffering, from a place of non-resistance just as easily as you can move into the world and change something or try to change something from resistance. Why do it from a place of closure and a place of suffering when you don't need to do that?

~

S: If one's occupation requires the individual to contract in order to continue, does this limit the potential for higher consciousness in personal life?

V: I would love to know what job or career creates contraction in a person or creates an environment where they have to contract because I haven't found any reason to contract or resist anything in 22 years and I'm involved with a great deal of people running many projects. So I'd love to know what career or occupation is that you feel that contraction is necessary.

~

S: I find that I often contract because of my beliefs in what's right and what's wrong. How do you remove the belief in right and wrong?

V: The only true way I know how not to have the belief in right and wrong is to know yourself as the universe and see clearly that perfection upon perfection upon perfection that actually is. I don't know another way.

~

S: Some definitions of superconsciousness that I've seen involve accessing a higher self. Do you think there is a higher self?

V: Look, if there is one, I haven't found it. I don't think there can be anything higher than knowing yourself as the universe, knowing yourself as nothing, knowing yourself as everything. I don't think there can be anything higher than that.

In my experience, there is no higher self. There is the mind and it thinks it's you. Then there is that that's aware of the mind, your true nature. And when that becomes aware of itself, there is the knowing of self as that, everything and nothing. This higher self I have never met.

~

S: Is there any significance of wearing different coloured clothes? Why do you wear white when doing Satsang?

V: White is the sattvic colour or a colour of purity. In Hindu religions, they have an understanding of the three gunas, the three types of energy field that different things can carry and produce, one being tamas, one being rajas, and one being sattvic. Now they divide these three gunas into ways to help towards awakening. The different foods you eat, the different clothes or colours you wear, the type of music you listen to. It's right through the culture. So the Hindu religion has injected into its culture an understanding that will support higher consciousness and awakening in just about every aspect of life, and of course, Buddhism came from Hinduism.

My understanding of the colour white is that it is the sattvic colour, and that it is clean and fresh and clear. And so I prefer to wear white when I'm holding

Satsang because it is a colour that gives a little percentage towards higher consciousness, the same as the food you eat gives a little percentage towards higher consciousness, the same as music or pretty much anything has somewhat of these three gunas in it, these three different types of energy: tamas being that lower consciousness energy that's kind of muddy and murky and unconscious, rajas being active or anxious or movement, and sattvic being pristine, clear, still.

So the idea is to go to sattvic. The idea is to become sattvic in mind, which you could say would be an equanimous mind, a mind that stays still even when being fired at. This sort of mind supports Enlightenment. And so I look for the advantages for people. What will help, even if it's only a small percentage? What will help in raising their consciousness levels, including the colour of their clothes?

~

S: I have heard you say the best meditation is watching the mind. However, I previously understood the Buddha taught to watch bodily sensations, like in vipassana meditation. Did the Buddha teach one or both? Thank you.

V: The Buddha taught both because the Buddha was a scientist of the mind. In watching the body, what is real? That's present moment awareness training. In witnessing the mind, we are seeing how it gets us caught in lower consciousness and because we can see it from a detached space, we don't need to get involved with it. Having detachment from the mind as a result of witnessing the mind is really good. It's really, really good because you don't get caught in it. So both methods – watching the body or watching the breath, and watching the mind – are very effective tools towards higher consciousness and Enlightenment.

~

S: What's the most common obstacle for people to access superconsciousness?

V: Oddly enough, if you're into higher consciousness, the most common obstacle – and it's hard to imagine – is collecting knowledge. We went to school and we collected knowledge and got our marks for getting answers right about that collected knowledge, so we went on to higher consciousness to think that we could do it the same way and it's just not true. No amount of collected knowledge will raise your consciousness levels. The same is that no amount of collected knowledge will heal a wound of the Heart. It just doesn't work that way.

What works are the practices. The practice of meditation, the practice of watching the breath, the practice of watching the mind or being a witness to the mind, the practice of self-inquiry, and the practice of openness work. These practices raise your consciousness levels.

The collection of knowledge cannot do that. It just makes you knowledgeable. So I would say that the greatest thing in the way of any seeker is the collection of knowledge because it makes us think that we're getting somewhere when we are not. You have to develop a beginner's mind and a beginner's mind does not know.

~

S: Do you think that too much sexual activity can keep me stuck in lower consciousness as it is associated with lower chakras?

V: Well the question begs to be asked, what is too much sexual activity? Oh really! I'm not against nature. Not at all. Nature is nature. Sexual activity can be used to raise consciousness levels. It's probably the hardest thing to use to raise consciousness levels, but it can be. By being 100 per cent present in the act of lovemaking, to what is, one develops present moment awareness and intimacy with the other.

But can you be 100 per cent present during lovemaking? Can you be totally with what is? It's a bit of a task. People tend to get into a bit of dream when they get into lovemaking and that kills all intimacy anyway because dreams can't really meet. When you truly meet another human being in lovemaking by being 100 per cent present to them, you melt as an "I" and you find yourself as one. And this is very beautiful. This is called tantra.

~

S: How do you know that everything is slowly evolving towards higher consciousness, as you said? Does this mean we don't need to do anything, and we're going to eventually get to Enlightenment?

V: Possibly. That's possibly true. The reason I say that everything is being reincarnated is because that is my own direct experience. The memories of lifetime after lifetime after lifetime after lifetime after lifetime – hundreds of lifetimes – so I know that reincarnations are real because I remember them.

I started remembering them when I was about 12 years old. I was a Catholic boarding school boy so it was a bit weird because in Catholicism you only have one life. So I was having quite a struggle at that time with what I was remembering. But it was so. We have lived many times before in many forms.

S: Is it a worthy pursuit to try and remember past lives?

V: Not really. The only thing that I got from past lives after witnessing hundreds of them was that you don't want to do this again. Samsara is the cycle of birth, life, death and reincarnation and birth again. It's basically painful. People suffer during their lives until they die. Basically, because life is dissatisfying, we constantly desire things to be different than how they are, which is suffering.

We get attached to the things that we feel we love and then we get fearful of losing them. This is suffering. This happens to all humans. This cycle of samsara can be ended through Enlightenment, knowing yourself as Truth. The ego dies before the body does. This is freedom, nirvana.

~

S: You said pain is the reason to avoid the cycle of samsara, but shouldn't we be okay with the pain?

V: It's not really pain. It's like, if you're going around the block in a motor car, or just walking around the block, and you just do it continuously, how long do you reckon it takes before you get a bit tired of doing it? It's not really about avoidance of pain. It's just that if you're not awake, you are living as something that you're not. You're not ego. You're not this thought structure that thinks it has a past and a future. That's a dream. You are pure awareness and you are here now.

If you can find a way as a mind to support that, awareness knowing itself, there is liberation. It's a worthy cause. If you wake up in this lifetime, if awareness becomes aware of itself in you in this lifetime, you become a light so others can see. It's very beautiful.

S: Is this being tired-of-going-around-the-block feeling enough of a motivator to take one to liberation? It wasn't for me.

V: I was curious. I just wanted to know what was at the top, and once I discovered what was at the top of the mountain, I wanted to stay there. My mind fell in love with Beingness and fell in love with Truth. It became willing to do whatever it took to support that because home is where your love is. My love was with Truth.

~

S: Is the perception of energies a sign of higher consciousness?

V: Not necessarily. It just means there's a certain part of you that's open that allows you to perceive them. I think that babies perceive everything, and as they get overwhelmed, or they get affected by it, they develop defence systems that stop them from perceiving because it can be too much.

Someone can get cracked open through trauma and start perceiving energies so it doesn't necessarily mean they have higher consciousness. They could just be damaged.

~

S: What happened in your life to contribute most to raising your consciousness levels?

V: Oddly enough, it wasn't anything spiritual. It was a need to survive. I grew up in a rather violent environment as a kid in a boarding school and unless I was switched on to what was happening around me all of the time it was dangerous. So I developed present moment awareness of what was real, what was actually happening around me, at quite a young age, which I kept through my adult years.

When I found meditation, I found it very easy, because I was already very present as a result of being switched on by being in a dangerous boarding school. When I look at higher consciousness – because part of higher consciousness is being switched on to reality – it was initiated by a dangerous environment at school and my need to be present to what was happening around me. If you are present to reality, if you are present to what's happening around you, you're in meditation. Not a bad start.

~

S: I love Truth and see the value in higher consciousness, but struggle with the practicalities of going through the dark night of the soul and trying to be in the marketplace, work, raise a family, etc. How did you manage it all?

V: Well, I also raised a family. I raised two families because I had split. I separated from one previously. I raised three children altogether, and I worked continuously as a naturopath and psychotherapist while going through the dark night of the soul, while going through all of the different things that had been trapped in my body, and undoing all of the different belief systems that created suffering in me. This was all done while working, while raising a family and in the marketplace.

This is why I teach the way I teach because there are methodologies that are great if you're in a monastery or if you're a monk or a nun somewhere in an ashram, but they don't work in the marketplace. What's required in the marketplace is a little different. I found that I had to practise openness, and that supported Heart, while at the same time practising meditation and self-inquiry. Two disciplines.

The practice of openness allowed me to be in my Heart, and because I was in my Heart, I could deal with the "dark night of the soul". So that was like one wing, the wing of devotion, the wing of the Heart. The other wing in the marketplace was that of discipline, meditation and self-inquiry. So I did these three practices and they gave me two wings to fly in the marketplace.

If you're practising openness, you actually have to find a way to accept life. Otherwise you can't stay open. That's just how it is. If you're practising meditation, you can see the different things that are contracting you. You can see the belief systems that are involved because you're witnessing the mind. So you can undo these things.

If you're practising self-inquiry, you can start turning awareness back onto itself and fall in love with Truth. This is the way this works in the marketplace. So it's a bhakti and a jnani path – not just a jnani path, not just a bhakti path, but a combination of the two that actually work in the marketplace. And I have never told anyone that it is easy. It is difficult. But higher consciousness is the best game in town. It's worth going for.

~

S: How did your Heart help you through the dark night of the soul?
V: It allowed me to have compassion for myself. And in that compassion, I could hold myself in tenderness while things weren't going well, when I was seeing things about myself that I didn't necessarily like. When I'd seen my own brokenness, and having to feel the pain of repressed emotions, being able to hold myself with love made it easier. To be tenderly okay with whatever appears demands a level of Heart, and if we really want to heal the wounds of our Heart, holding ourselves in tenderness is the way.

~

S: Are there different levels of higher consciousness that you must access before living in superconsciousness?
V: Some people say so. I don't think so. Higher consciousness basically means you can see through the mind and you're not getting caught in it anymore. That's the bottom line. You've seen through the mind. You've seen all of the belief systems. You've seen all of the defences. You've undone the mind and you're not contracting to life anymore because you can see it all clearly and it's all been undone. This is higher consciousness.

Superconsciousness is very different. It's knowing yourself as Truth, which is beyond the mind. It's up to you. Higher consciousness is difficult, but it is pretty much a necessity before superconsciousness. People can get glimpses of superconsciousness before Enlightenment. But it's unlikely to stay if they haven't done the work to create higher consciousness in their own minds.

~

S: Often I'll get caught in constant doing, from the time I get up to when I go to bed, feeling happy at times, but sometimes, it also makes me stressed and unconscious. Is this constant doing in the way of higher consciousness?

V: Yeah, it is. It is. To gain higher consciousness, you need to be able to be still, you need to be able to be silent so you can see properly. While you're constantly doing, you're distracting yourself. More than likely, you're distracting yourself from feeling something. But it could have become a lifelong habit of do-aholism. There's lots of different ways to escape wounding that we have inside, and one of them is do-aholism. Alcoholism, drug taking, gaming, food – there's so many ways. But can you be still? Can you be quiet? Then just see what happens. Just watch the mind. Can you be like a stone and not move, just witness? This will show you where you're at.

~

S: Sometimes I feel a sense of pointlessness when it comes to striving for higher consciousness because it's not easy. What is your motivation to help people to higher consciousness and to access superconsciousness?

V: Compassion, born from love. There is no other motivation. When you love people – and that's what happens when you're Heart awakens, you just love people – you love everyone. You want to take care of them. You want to help them in some way. For most people, you can't help too much because they're not seekers. They're unconscious to that, but you can light them up, you can take away some of the pain. But the motivator? There is no other motivator but love. Because of love, you just want to take care of everybody and everything because this is how love affects the mind. It's very beautiful.

It does kind of demand that you get out of the way because you tend to be the obstacle. You tend to be the one who keeps contracting and cutting yourself off from your own Heart. Openness supports Heart. Being undefended supports Heart. Being vulnerable supports Heart.

What stops you from perceiving Heart is defensiveness and closure, contraction, resistance. So the Way of the Heart in a lot of ways is the path of least resistance. And it's beautiful. It'll motivate you to take care. You see, if the whole world had Heart, we wouldn't have any wars. We wouldn't have any terrorists. We wouldn't have any murders and we wouldn't have any rapes. We wouldn't have any theft. We wouldn't have any starvation because everybody would be taking care of everybody.

The problem with this world is there isn't enough Heart. But you can make a difference. You can open up. You can drop your defences. You can awaken as Heart. It's up to you.

~

S: Do superconsciousness and Heart always go together?

V: You can go directly to super consciousness through self-inquiry and bypass Heart, but if you stay in super consciousness, it's likely that the Heart's likely to open anyway because to be in superconsciousness, the mind is in a state of surrender which is the right ground for Heart too.

Some people find Heart before awakening. You can wake up Heart as an ego, simply by being out of the way, simply by being wide open, simply by being vulnerable. Or you can wake up to Truth and not have Heart because you've used self-inquiry as a methodology towards Heart. But after awakening, you'll find Heart because after awakening there's nothing in the way anymore. All of the obstacles are gone. You're just wide open, and then Heart appears and affects the mind in such a way that you just want to take care of everything and everyone. This is the Beauty Way.

~

S: If in a previous life I had done a lot of work towards higher consciousness, would it be easier in this life?

V: Heck yeah! We carry our credit and our debit life to life, so we carry our good karma and our bad karma from life to life. This is why if you go into any Buddhist monastery and ask the abbot, "What can I do towards Enlightenment?" they'll say "Become a generous person, take care of others, be kind, be gentle" because this accrues good karma.

Anytime we're involved in something that hurts others or ourselves, we're accruing negative karma. This karmic credit and karmic debt comes in lifetime after lifetime after lifetime. People think, well, I'm suffering a great deal in this life, why is that? Well, maybe you're paying something back from a previous life. Or maybe you're doing very well in this lifetime, your consciousness levels are going through the roof and you don't really know why because you haven't done that much. You're carrying credit from a previous life and that credit is paying out. Some people are born awake. I haven't met one yet, but I've heard of them. Well, if they're born awake, and they stay awake, that's just a carry on from a previous life. I heard Amma Mother was born awake. That would be a result of previous lifetimes of work. It's all karmic.

~

S: Does your ego have to be completely destroyed in order to have superconsciousness?

V: Completely destroyed? I don't think so. It's the story of you that usually is a problem. If there isn't a story of you, there isn't a problem. In Buddhism, sometimes they say "no I, no problem". But it doesn't need to be destroyed. It just needs to learn acceptance and surrender. I mean, if you really look at it, what you need to learn, that's it.

The only thing a human being needs to learn towards higher consciousness is acceptance and surrender. If we're in acceptance, we don't resist life. We don't contract to life, we support life. If we're in acceptance of life, we're wide open and we're now supporting Heart.

It's very beautiful. The only thing that a spiritual seeker really needs to learn is openness. Openness counts for everything. In practising openness, we are practising the true revolution against the contracting, defended mind. This is the revolution.

~

S: Are there any indicators that can tell me I'm going in the right direction towards higher consciousness?
V: It's difficult, because quite often when people get into higher consciousness, they go into the dark night of the soul and it feels like they're going the wrong way. Everything inside of them says "no, you're going the wrong way" because it's so uncomfortable. And this is where being with others who are into higher consciousness helps – being in a community of people who are going for higher consciousness or with someone who has higher consciousness – because they will support you in going in the right direction. We are programmed primarily to avoid pain and chase pleasure. And of course, if we're into healing the wounds of our Heart, if we're into undoing the belief systems of our mind, this is going to be hard. It's going to be uncomfortable. It goes against primal programming.

It's always best if you're into higher consciousness to hang out with people who are also into higher consciousness, going in the same direction as you. I chose teachers who could see me and who were prepared to tell me what they could see. I wasn't interested in being told how lovely I was or how well I was doing. I was interested in seeing the obstacles that were in my way, and my teachers, particularly a man called Teertha, who was one of Osho Rajneesh's therapists, was particularly good at this, and I did a lot of work with him in the 80s.

It's up to you, though. It's difficult. I had a great deal of help. I had teachers the whole way through, showing me the way. I think if you try doing it by yourself, the ego will find a way to avoid because it is such a defensive, protective entity. It's good to be in the company of people going the same direction who will help you and support you in that.

People who aren't into higher consciousness won't support you. They don't have the ability to. They don't even know where you're going. They don't even know what you're doing. They don't understand it because if you're not into higher consciousness, you're probably just into being comfortable, whether that's through workaholism, food addiction, alcoholism, doing drugs, gaming, whatever, there's a myriad of different things. Those things are just medication really, people medicating themselves because they're uncomfortable.

If you're into higher consciousness, you can't really medicate yourself anymore. You've got to face the music, and it's difficult. That's why it's best done with people travelling in the same direction, with people who will support you.

~

S: Meditation is the main practice for Buddhism and other spiritual traditions. Can meditation alone take people into superconsciousness?

V: Look, I would say yes, but it has not been my direct experience. My direct experience tells me that self-inquiry can take you into higher consciousness or superconsciousness.

I can say that meditation allowed me to see through my mind, allowed me to see the obstacles and defence systems. It allowed me to witness the mind to see what games it was playing with me, how dishonest it was. And because it was seen, it could be undone. Meditation also allowed me to find a lot of peace, a lot of no-mind, but it didn't actually show me Truth.

What showed me Truth was self-inquiry, first done in the Zen practice of asking the question, "Who am I?" and discounting it, and then asking the question again for hours and hours on end; and second, the Advaita Vedanta methodology of self-inquiry, asking the question, "Who's aware?" or "Who am I" in an attempt to turn awareness back to itself. I found those two methodologies very helpful and effective in showing me who I truly was.

The other thing that really helped was sitting in the presence of my teachers. It was a bit of a gift. Towards the end, all I had to do was be in their presence and I was gone and Beingness was aware of itself, so I'm very grateful to those teachers – very grateful for those people who were willing to be lights for others and for me.

Meditation itself, a great tool, allowed me to see a great many things. And maybe people can find Enlightenment through it, but it has not been my own direct experience so I can't say yes. I say "I don't know". I advocate meditation as a practice towards higher consciousness and Enlightenment. I advocate self-inquiry and openness. These things all work.

Thank you for Satsang. Good to see you bravehearts here today.

CHAPTER TEN

Why Is Enlightenment An Inward Adventure?

S: Vishrant, can you please talk about wise Enlightenment and inward adventure?
V: The whole world is interested in the outside. The sage is interested in the inside. The mystic is interested in the inside and the seeker is interested in the inside because it is only on the inside that we find our true nature. We can't find it outside of ourselves. We can't see it. It's on the inside. It's that that is aware of the outside. But people are more interested in the outside because in the outside they can make money, they can get a house, and they can have a relationship. They can make things work in the material world, but it is only on the inside that we can find our true nature which is pure awareness.

I call it an inward adventure because it's an amazing adventure – or you can see it as something that's really hard. You know it's all attitudinal really. See, when we start looking on the inside, we start to find things that aren't so beautiful. We start to find our broken programming. We start to find our wounding, our pain bodies. We can also find Beingness.

It's an adventure to undo every obstacle that is in the way. It's an adventure to find the beauty of Heart. It's an adventure for awareness to turn onto itself.

It's an amazing adventure from the perspective of the mind. Or it can be seen as a trial, it can be seen as arduous. But really, it's just an adventure.

This adventure for me began when I was 19 when I got involved in encounter groups in Perth, Western Australia, and it was all about having a look at what was happening inside of me, how I was operating internally, and how that was affecting my external reality. Of course, in those days it was more about personal growth, but it set me on the track to having a look inside. It set me on the inward adventure.

Now I see the whole journey for people who come from ignorance to Enlightenment as an adventure, an inward adventure, and the best adventure there is because ultimately there is nothing to do here but wake up to our true nature and to exist as that rather than stay ignorant and live as an ego. The inward adventure facilitates that awakening, that Enlightenment.

Are there any questions, any statements, any challenges to this teaching today?

S: Is seeing it as an inward adventure just an attitude that you choose?

V: Yep, it's just an attitude. You can see it as something that's really difficult, something that is really a trial and something you don't want to do. Something that's uncomfortable. Or you can see it as an amazing adventure, which is what it is.

~

S: Did you ever feel limited in your spiritual journey by your family and professional obligations?

V: I tended to put Truth first. I tended to put the adventure first and that cost me because there's a price for putting your spiritual journey first. It is the price for higher consciousness because quite often the people who you're involved with, your family and your friends, even your partners, are not in support of your spiritual journey because it's not theirs, and maybe they're not even on one, and they don't understand what you're into. Over the years, different people who didn't want to be involved in the spiritual quest, didn't want to be involved in waking up and were more interested in making the material world work, have dropped away out of my life.

As far as money's concerned, well, when I was a seeker, there weren't any enlightened people in Australia that I knew of so I had to leave Australia and live in places like India and Italy and England and America with awake people, and that cost a lot. Financially, it was very expensive over the years. So there was a financial cost to the inward adventure as well. It's one of the reasons that I don't travel. I stay here in Perth so the people here don't have to go and follow gurus around the world in other places. So I don't move, I just stay here and people can come and they can sit with me. They don't have to pay exorbitant prices. They don't have to travel to another country. It's all home-grown here.

So it did cost a lot, really. Eventually I gave up my businesses completely because I saw that they were in the way of my journey, particularly my journey towards Heart, finding and perceiving Heart. As a businessman, I had hardened up. I'd closed up way too much. For me, I had to get out of business. I had to give my businesses away in the pursuit of Heart, and I did.

So it cost me numerous relationships and my business, money, prestige, reputation, but it was all worth it. It was all worth it. There is nothing worth doing here except raising your consciousness levels, becoming more and more aware of how the mind works, and eventually, ultimately aware of awareness itself and awareness staying aware of itself which is Enlightenment

~

S: What is the reason why someone would want to find themselves as Truth?
V: Unless you know that it's a possibility, you wouldn't. Most of the West, most Westerners have no idea what Enlightenment is. They have no idea whatsoever that they're actually imprisoned because Christianity has kept people ignorant. If people knew that there was a way out of their mind, if they knew there was a way to have continuous, profound contentment, they would probably go for it, but it's just not part of our society. Our society lives in the delusion that they are somebodies who have been somewhere and are going somewhere – that they are a body and a mind, and this is a delusion.

We are pure awareness. We cannot be anything other than pure awareness and we are always here, whether the mind is present or not. We were never born and we cannot die, but most people believe themselves to be a mind and a body. It's a belief, it's not a reality. When awareness turns on itself in a human being, the mind recognises what is real and what is not. It recognises that Beingness is real and "it" is not. It is just an appearance in what we truly are: pure Beingness, pure awareness.

Why would people try to find freedom if they don't realise they're imprisoned? Up until the age of 28, I didn't have a clue. It wasn't until I came in contact with Bhagwan Shree Rajneesh in America that I realised there was another possibility for human beings, that there were actually different types of people on the planet. Two types: those who are awake and those who are dreaming that they are somebody. There is no freedom in believing you are somebody. Take away your imagination and that somebody doesn't exist. What are we really? And can we actually live or exist as that? And the answer is yes. It's called Enlightenment.

~

S: Vishrant, since I've discovered you online, even now while I'm on this call, I can just feel my thoughts slipping away. I can feel the energy from you. I'm 57 years old and I've been seeking most of my life. I've had some glimpses and little awakenings along the way, but my burning question the last while has been, am I doing life or is it doing me? I'm trying to get into alignment with life so that it's living me rather than this personality living it. I find problems with discipline a little bit in that regard, because I'm trying to come into alignment with it. Is there anything that you could say in this regard for me?

V: This is just for you, it's not for everybody else. This is just for you. Give your life to Truth and start telling peo-

ple about it. What you have found, what you know, this is just for you. I feel quite strongly that if you start talking about what you know, to people, and you give your life to Truth, you'll find yourself living as Truth before long.
S: Thank you. Thank you. Thank you very much, sir. I appreciate that Vishrant.
V: If you have any more questions at any time, contact me again.
S: Thank you, Vishrant.

~

S: Hi Vishrant, I've been watching your videos and I had a question. I was wondering if you can guide me. I've been doing the dynamic meditation for more than a year now, and in the fourth stage of it, when I'm sitting there, I start with having thoughts that keep on coming and then after a while everything disappears and even I'm not there. I snap back from that state after some time and it feels like I was asleep. But I know it was not sleep, so I was just wondering if what I'm experiencing is what is known as no-mind or that is what meditation is?
V: Yeah, meditation is no-mind. You also could be experiencing a form of satori, where you go into the black nothingness. But you know that's very, very good. That's a waiting ground for Enlightenment. Have you tried self-inquiry?
S: I do. That is my evening or the second practice that I do during the day if I have a chance or else before bed. I practice self-inquiry where I sit, close my eyes, and I do self-inquiry.
V: Yes.

S: But I haven't moved past the identification that I have with myself in my mind. When I'm observing what I consider myself in my mind, that is the point where I'm not thinking, and I stay in that state for maybe I-don't-know-how-long and then I come back to thoughts again.
V: So what's happening in your mind right now, right at this moment?
S: I'm aware of who I think I am is looking at you.
V: Okay, so let's try that one again. What's happening inside your head right now?
S: Nothing. I'm just looking at you.
V: Yes, just looking. Okay. So now let's see what's looking. What's actually looking? Turn awareness back to itself. What's looking?
S: Maybe I'm the witness, the witness that I see. I always find that that's me.
V: Okay, it can't be a "maybe," it's got to be directly in the moment so you're looking at what's looking.

There's something looking at Vishrant. What's looking? Turn awareness back and see what's looking and see the qualities that this has. I'll give you some clues. First of all, you won't find anything. You'll just find a nothingness or an emptiness and that emptiness will be silent and still. Now you're looking in the right place for Beingness because Beingness doesn't move, doesn't make noise, and quite often, it appears as emptiness and nothingness.
S: My vision goes towards my third eye when I do that.
V: Yep, I understand. What's aware of the third eye? You turn it again, you see, you use the same question, what's aware of the third eye? Because your awareness

has gone to the third eye. Now, what's aware of that? Because that's also an experience, and experiences appear in who you are. What's aware of the third eye? What's this that's aware? What are its qualities? They're almost impossible to talk about because when you start turning awareness onto itself, you find there's a nothingness there or an emptiness there. You can, of course, find everything as self, but that's a different type of satori. Quite often, in the early stages of self-inquiry, you just find a blank, or a nothingness, an emptiness, which is very peaceful and it doesn't make noise and it doesn't move. And because we're not trained to look at that, because we're trained to look for things that move and make noise, we miss this background that is always here. So as a meditator, you're finding no-mind. Beautiful. "What's aware of no-mind?" is a really good question. What's aware? What's aware? What's aware?

S: I really don't have an answer for you, it is just ... it's just a feeling.

V: Ah, you can't come up with an answer.

S: It's just a feeling.

V: Yep, so now you're looking in the right direction.

S: Okay, it's just a witness that is looking at things.

V: Yes, yes. Keep looking at the witness. Keep turning awareness, the witness, back onto itself. Keep turning awareness back to itself and you will find that you are that and you always have been that.

S: Okay.

V: This methodology does work. Keep turning awareness back to what you become aware of. So you became aware of the third eye. What's aware of the third eye? What is witnessing the third eye? That's of interest. The third eye itself is just an experience. What's aware of it is who you truly are.

S: Okay.

V: It's nice to talk to you.

S: Same here. So you're suggesting I should just continue inquiring and keeping focus on attention of who's aware?

V: Your meditations have taken you to a reasonably good place and it's time for you to use self-inquiry as a methodology to turn awareness back to itself – for the witness to become aware of itself.

S: Okay, thanks. I do live in the world, and have family and stuff, so sometimes I get scared of being non-functional or finally finding something that I'm looking for. How do I let go of that?

V: Just keep self-inquiring. You've got to remember that in my own journey, I was a family man. I had three children and a wife and another family that I took care of. And I ran my own business as a naturopath and psychotherapist. And I did all of these things while self-inquiring, while asking the question "Who's aware?" Also, I was a meditator like you, so meditation and self-inquiry and the practice of openness were my way of life of being in the world. And I did that while in the marketplace. Don't worry about anything, just keep self-inquiring as to who's aware. The worry just brings you back to the mind and living as worry. Because whatever we put our awareness on, we live as. So if you're worrying about how it's going to affect you, you live as worry. Just keep turning awareness back to itself and see where that takes you. It'll take you home to your true nature. And then you can still operate in the world, but you'll operate differently because you operate from Being-based reality rather than ego-based reality. And for you, I don't know what that's going to look like. But if you're interested in Enlightenment, keep self-inquiring.

~

S: You're speaking of different types of satoris. Is there a way to facilitate deeper satoris?

V: Just turn awareness back to itself. Finding Beingness or finding awareness, pure awareness, at first it's like walking around an abyss that you're watching, because there's nothing there. It's a great big abyss. No borders, no boundaries, silent and still, and you're walking around and you're watching this abyss. If you keep watching the abyss at some point you discover you are the abyss. You don't need to worry about different depths of satoris or even whether you're having one. Just keep turning awareness back to itself until there is nothing left, just pure awareness aware of itself.

~

S: Hello Vishrant.

V: Hello.

S: My whole body is shaking, I'm so excited to talk to you. It's just like something's triggered within me. I've been searching for Truth my whole life, or pretty close to it, and your advice to me to speak to people – it's funny lately, I've become almost very quiet and only speaking when life tells me "Okay, you can say something to this person" or whatever.

But I was very blessed. I was a cameraman and I worked for CNN International in London and it took me all over the world, and I saw, I saw love from so many different angles, and I've got to a point now where I really just want, I just feel I need to surrender, because I'm seeing patterns. It's like life talks to me. It talks to me through patterns and almost synchronicities that are magical. But I do feel as I get out of alignment with these patterns that my old beliefs and everything kick in slightly and cause fear and anxiety. So sorry, this is a long-winded thing, but just basically if I talk to people, where would that come from? Would that just come from just surrendering and letting it come? I'm not even sure of the question. I think you know what I mean?

V: As a cameraman – because I was a cameraman also, that's how I got to interview Osho Rajneesh and take a lot of photographs of him. I was a photojournalist also – when you're taking that shot, you have to go silent and still inside before you press the trigger, particularly when you're using film. Now, the way to talk to people about Truth is that same space of silence and stillness. Just before you take the shot, making sure that everything's in frame, that lighting's right, the speed of the film's right, the shutter speed is right, the aperture is right. And then you talk, from that space of absolutely nothing, just before you fire that camera. Do you know that space I'm talking about?

S: Absolutely, because there's times when I'm shooting where it just feels like it absorbs me into the image so that it's like I'm shooting, but it's just moving me around while I'm framing and getting the action.
V: Yes, and when I was taking photographs of Osho, his energy was affecting my mind so my mind would stop. Now Osho was aware that I was taking the photo, and he would stay still for me so I could take the shot. My mind stopped, and I couldn't take the shot, so he would stay still. I would stay still. [LAUGHTER]
S: Wow. Thank you. I so appreciate it. It's so wonderful meeting you.
V: It's lovely to meet you. I've met you deeper than you can know.
S: Thank you.

~

S: Is the inward adventure necessarily a solo journey?
V: Absolutely a solo journey. You can't take anyone with you. People can walk on the path with you, but they can't come inside with you. They can support you on the outside, but they can't come inside with you. That's not possible. But what happens when you find self, when you find true self, you find that there were never two people anyway, there was only one being. We are all one. So this solo journey inward takes us to knowing ourselves as everything and everyone: only one.
S: Does the inward adventure have to be a hard and long process?
V: It doesn't have to be any way. It just has to happen the way it's going to happen. You have to learn to get

out of the way and allow it to happen. Your trying to control is in the way. You don't know how much pain body you have. You don't know how much karma you may need to pay back or be rewarded with. You don't know. It's very much an unknown inward adventure, an unknown journey, and you have to be okay with "I don't know". It may be hard. It may not be hard. But the key is acceptance of everything as it is. That's the key.

S: Would everyone's inward journey lead to the same Truth?

V: Yes, there is only one Truth. There is only one Beingness. There are not two Beingnesses. That that is aware is the same in everybody. It's like no matter where you go around the world, if you taste the ocean, it will be salty. Beingness is always the same, like the ocean. There are not two varieties or three varieties of Beingness. There's one variety and it is everything.

S: Once you start the inward journey, can you take a break or stop, or does it have to be a daily commitment?

V: You can do whatever you like. You can stop, you can start, you can continue. My understanding is that if you do begin, don't stop. You'll be disgruntled because once you've begun, you start to discover things are very different than what we've been taught at school, what our religions tell us, what our governments tell us. You find there's a whole other realm of Truth and a lot of the belief systems that you were handed by the way you were brought up by your government, your church, aren't actually true. So if you stop the journey, you kind of get disgruntled because you know too much. You're better off finishing the journey once you've started it.

~

S: My desire to find a partner keeps pulling me away from the present moment. I start dreaming more. What would you recommend me to do with that desire?

V: Find a partner. If you want to find a partner, find a partner. If you want to have a job, have a job. If you don't want to have a job, don't have a job. Follow what you want. The best want is the want to know yourself as Truth. That's the best one.

When we look at desires, they all make us unhappy because if we have a desire for something to be different, we're not happy. We're in a state of discontentment. So if we're going to have states of discontentment, why don't we just have one state of discontentment – and that would be the desire to wake up – and give that desire to wake up your totality. Anything that human beings give their totality to usually succeeds. It's up to you. If on the way to Enlightenment, or with that desire to wake up, you decide to do all of these other things, well, you're probably going to get lost. Because whatever you put your awareness into is where you live. It's up to you. I encourage people to go for Truth because it's the only freedom.

~

S: With self-inquiry, how will I find out that I have come home? Will I ever find out?

V: Once you come home, you will not be asking me that question because the difference between knowing self as pure awareness and knowing self as an ego is so vastly different it cannot be missed. In ego-based reality, you have all these reference points that make the ego up from the past projected to the future and a whole pile of belief systems. In Beingness, in pure awareness, there are no reference points. Vastly different.

~

S: I've gone through quite a lot of Osho's literature, and in that literature, he talks about taking a jump or leap. If you have heard about it and know about it, can you elaborate on that?

V: Yeah. Awareness is mostly aware of the mind, and through the senses, the world, for most human beings. For the sage who's awake, awareness is aware of itself and can also be aware of the mind and the world through the senses.

The leap is the leap from having awareness just on the mind and through the senses to being on itself. That is the leap.

S: How do we take that leap? Is self-inquiry the way?

V: Yeah, this is the thing: people are looking for an instant result, and really, you just have to self-inquire and self-inquire and self-inquire. Then an accident happens when you're least expecting it, when you're least guarded, an accident happens. That accident is when awareness finds itself, which is satori. If it stays on itself permanently, it's Enlightenment.

What you as a mind can do, what you as an ego can do, is set up for that accident, produce the right ground for the accident to occur in, and the right ground for the accident of Enlightenment to occur is meditation and self-inquiry.

~

S: You said in some of your earlier talks that when awareness became aware of itself, it was like two magnets coming together. Now, when I feel Truth, like real Truth, and I've studied Osho as well as travelled around with some so-called enlightened masters all over the world and searched and various things, but when I feel that Buddha field, as you talk of it, I feel it very, very strongly now. There's this magnetic pull that is also feeling like it brings up all of my other stuff as well that's still residue, and it's very, very painful as well, and that makes me feel very awkward and weird.

My mind is just going away while I'm talking to you. What I wanted to ask is: I'm aware that there is this repeated cycle of trying to reach this point of Truth. You describe it as many lives. I've tried to remember my lives. I haven't been able to, but I do feel like I've been going round and round in the cycle many, many times. But what goes around? I mean, if "me" is an illusion? When I die, what comes back and what keeps searching again? I'm sorry that I've been a bit vague. I'm just feeling your presence and it's so overwhelming right now Vishrant.

V: So, I'm going to answer the question that was underneath all of that. The pain body that's there, the uncomfortable feelings inside that have been there for this life and maybe other lifetimes will come to the surface when you come into the presence of someone who's awake or when you start self-inquiring. As Jung put it, the dark night of the soul occurs. And the only thing that you can offer that will assist that is your warm welcoming – your warm acceptance of what is. Nothing else.

In that warm acceptance, we learn surrender. That's how we learn surrender, and it is surrender that will facilitate Enlightenment. It's like a human being is like a worm on a hot tin roof, flipping from side to side trying to find comfort. When you as the worm decide to just lay on that tin roof and burn in acceptance, you're setting yourself up for Enlightenment, because now you've surrendered. People think that when they accept, the pain will go away. No, the pain doesn't go away, but the resistance to the pain goes away.

S: It almost feels like a very fast vibration, trying to get into that frequency, and it's just slightly out and it's almost wobbling really, really fast. And I'm just wanting to let everything go, but there's still this little part of me that's just going "No, I've got a wife, I've got a job". I work as a rigger now in the film industry and it's hard because there are a lot of rough characters as well. It's not all smooth sailing because you've got to deal with them.

V: Just for a second, look at me now as though you're looking through the lens of a camera and you're about to take that shot where you have to be silent and still, and watch how your mind just backs off. This is the way to be with me. Can you feel it?

S: I can.

V: This is the right ground. When your mind backs off, you're putting yourself in the right space for everything.

~

S: Do most people who find and dwell in Beingness end up going all of the way to Enlightenment?

V: No, most people don't. Most people don't. There's something that people miss. They don't recognise that someone who's enlightened has given their life to Truth. They actually don't really have a life anymore for themselves. It's over. The ego-mind has given itself to Truth, and in that it has died, it is surrendered unconditionally. Those who are fully awake serve Truth and they may serve Heart, but they don't serve themselves. That's over, that's gone. That's ended.

Not many people wake up because they're not willing to give their life to Truth. They want to wake up and they want to have something for themselves. Well, that's not the deal. The deal is very simple: everything for Truth and nothing for you; or everything for Heart and nothing for you. They're the only deals that work. There is no deal where the ego gets to wake up. It never wakes up. It surrenders unconditionally and that that's aware of it stays aware of itself. Very different. And then the mind facilitates that by being in service to that.

~

S: The following question is from a viewer: Is desire the same as yang energy?

V: Look, outgoing energy is yang energy. Yin energy is just receptivity. It's just a wide, wide openness, allowing everything to pass through. It is so beautiful. Yang energy is outgoing. If you like, yang energy is in the way. You need to become yin.

They say in some religions in India that those who have awakened are all women because even if they're men in body, they became women because they've become absolutely receptive, absolutely yin. Everything that was in the way has been surrendered and now the world flows through them rather than gets caught in them.

~

S: What about desire to be healed from a continuous, debilitating migraine? How can one even continue to meditate?

V: Yeah, bad news. I only have one answer and that's acceptance. There is no magical answer that is going to help you. Acceptance is the only answer that works – and medication. See, people want something different. They want an answer that will relieve them of pain. But really, the key to freedom, the key to Enlightenment is unconditional surrender, and we learn unconditional surrender, which is a non-doing, by the practice of acceptance of what is.

Can your mind accept the headache or is it going into resistance? In acceptance, the mind can rest in the pain. In non-acceptance, the mind will resist the pain and suffer.

Eight weeks ago, on Sunday, I had a motorbike accident, and for seven weeks, I've been in pain, continuous pain, because four ribs got broken and my collarbone got broken. Absolute total acceptance of the pain didn't change the pain, but there was no suffering because there was no resistance to the pain. This is something that really needs to be practised to be understood: the practice of accepting what is without reservation – if anything, a warm welcoming of what is. Your choice. Pain is pain. It is our resistance to pain that is suffering. The mind probably wants another answer because it wants pain relief, but the key to Enlightenment is acceptance. In acceptance, there is no more story, there is no more you. It is over. Perfect.

S: What is it that makes you know too much to go back to living a life of happy, mundane ignorance?

V: So, I was brought up a Roman Catholic. I did 12 years in a Catholic school. I was led to believe a whole pile of things by my government, by my peers, by my teachers. Upon examination, I found that they weren't true, so I decided to adventure and find out what was true. The more that I saw that was true and the more that I saw that what I'd been programmed to believe wasn't true, the less chance I had of going back to what I was like before, because what I was like before was very much based on all of these belief systems that weren't real.

I started to realise that there was something here that was greater than the "I", Beingness, and I just couldn't go back to living as an "I" and be satisfied – completely satisfied with living as an "I" when I knew there was something else, when I knew that I was something else. The only way that you can probably do that is to stay drunk or something, stoned, but how long can you do that for? Go for Truth. Go for the totality of who you truly are. Turn awareness onto itself and be free, and be free and be free. In that, you get to see that you are never ever imprisoned, that there was no such thing as freedom, because Beingness has always been here. You are just unaware of it. But you are always at your final destination, here.

~

S: Sometimes, I'll be 70 per cent in Beingness and 30 per cent doing something simple. After a while, I'll be unable to exactly account for the last couple of minutes. Does this necessarily mean I was out of it, then?

V: I love the way you could measure it. That's amazing, putting a percentage on how much you're in and how much you're out. Right now, my awareness is out here with you to some degree. It's also inside on itself to some degree, and because I can still talk, it must be out here to some degree to a fair percentage, I guess, because when it goes in, all language is lost, just silence and stillness. But does it really matter? Does it really matter? Just keep turning awareness back to itself.

All of these questions, like this one to understand, are in effect some form of wanting to control. Let go of control completely and trust. Self-inquire, "Who am I? What is aware?" and trust. See where that trust takes you. The controlling mind has to let go because it's in the way. The best answer that you can ever come up with is "I don't know" because there's no control in that. The quest to know things is also the quest to control things. It is the ego and its survival mechanism that wants to control. Let go, let go, let go. Let go of everything and be free.

~

S: How would the mind surrender itself because the question also arises from the mind?

V: When you look at surrender, or unconditional surrender, it's actually a non-doing, and the mind can't do unconditional surrender. It actually has to be programmed for that to occur, and it gets programmed for that to occur through the practice of acceptance, the practice of putting yourself aside. If we just look at the Buddhist meditation of watching the breath, you're watching the breath, the mind comes in, you let the mind go, you come back to the breath. You're actually practising surrendering the mind. So meditation, the practice of watching the breath is a practice of learning to let the mind go over and over again when it comes back into play. Self-inquiry, asking what's aware, is another practice of letting the mind go because you're not trying to look in the mind, you're trying to find what's aware. The mind cannot do unconditional surrender, but it can be trained for that to occur.

Unconditional surrender works like this: you insult me, and nothing moves. That's unconditional surrender. It's not a doing. It's a non-doing. Nothing moves. This is hard for the ego to understand, because it likes to be able to do things, it likes to be able to manufacture things, but it can't really manufacture unconditional surrender. All it can do is practise acceptance, meditation, and eventually there is non-doing, non-reacting. Now you have a mind that is equanimous: a mind that will support Enlightenment.

~

S: Hello Vishrant. So while I'm out and about at my job, doing problem solving, in those moments, how would you suggest I go about it? If I'm doing self-inquiry while I'm doing my tasks, then I'm not focused on my tasks and my tasks require my attention to be outwardly focused. So how do I go about being? Being in those situations where I have to perform tasks where my attention needs to be on something outside of me? Or do I come back to self-inquiry periodically when I can think of it? how would you suggest I be in those situations?

V: What is your job?

S: I'm a software developer. I write computer programs.

V: Ah yes, I understand. Okay, so here, here we go with this one, this will blow your mind. After awakening 22 years ago, I decided that I'd put a website together to promote Satsang. I worked on it for three days straight without sleep because the program kept failing because it was faulty. At no point did awareness leave awareness and at no point did I get caught in the mind. Yet I was able to put a website together from no-mind. The reason was that my mind had previously been programmed to be a mechanic and to work on computers. I knew it all. I didn't have to think about it. It all happened automatically, very much similar to riding a bike. Admittedly, it was slower than if I was using my rational mind, but it all happened by itself without me getting too involved at all in it and thinking. I just waited for the answers and the answers would come because my mind had already been programmed.

Your mind has probably already been programmed to do a lot of what you do. It happens a little bit automatically, similar to riding a pushbike. Check it out. We only think we need to think. A lot of what we do, we don't need to think about at all. We can just do it. How's that sound?

S: It sounds really out there because I haven't done it myself.

V: Try, try. You must have a fair bit of knowledge about computers by now because that's your job. Try doing a lot of it without thinking. Try just staying in no-mind and just doing it and watch what happens. Watch how efficient and effective you can be, but you have to trust. Your mind has to trust. And see what happens.

S: Okay, thanks.

V: When you were a little boy, the same as me, we had to learn a lot of different things. Then we had to go to school and learn a lot of things. Then we had to go to secondary school and learn a lot of things. But once we've learnt them, we've learnt them, like riding a pushbike. We don't need to think about riding a pushbike. Once we've ridden it, we just ride it.

A lot of the things we do, including mechanics, including computer science, can be done automatically because we've already learned it.

S: Can I ask a little follow up on that, then? Yeah. How would you suggest tackling something that you're learning or you're doing it for the first time?

V: That's a little different. But you've got to remember, I was putting a website together for the first time.
S: Okay.
V: Ah, look, if I have to transfer money from one bank account to another account and I'm not familiar with what's going on, a certain level of involvement's required, but only for a few seconds. And then bang, back to nothing. You'd be surprised at how much you can actually do without thinking just because your mind is already programmed to do it. Now, if you had never been trained, or you'd never practised in what you're doing, well, you wouldn't be good at it, you wouldn't be able to do it, you'd have to learn it. But you know most of it already, probably all of it, because you've done it so many times before.

This is my life nowadays and has been for 22 years. I don't live in my head. When I stop talking, my mind is silent. There is no editor that stops things coming out of my mouth, it is just straight. A lifetime of being in the world before awakening – and for you the same, you have so much expertise. You'll be surprised at how much you don't have to think when you really just allow yourself to be with what it is. You'll see all of the answers rather than think about them. You'll know all of the answers without thinking. Check it out.

Get back to me. Let me know how you go with that. I'd love to hear.
S: Okay, I'll let you know how it goes. Thank you.
V: Thank you. Thank you for Satsang. Good to see you bravehearts here today.

CHAPTER ELEVEN

Why Higher Consciousness Is So Hard

V: Everyone gets born into lower consciousness. The animals are in lower consciousness. Our primal imperative to survive is basically lower consciousness, so to go from lower consciousness to higher consciousness we have to challenge primal programming, the programming to survive, because it keeps us locked in lower consciousness. The other thing with adult humans is we nearly all went to school and learnt to live in our heads so we could pass exams by repeating answers to get a diploma or a degree or something. We learned to live in our heads to do that and never ever recovered from doing that, and of course living in your head or dreaming or thinking constantly keeps you in lower consciousness also.

This is why if you go into any Buddhist monastery anywhere in the world the first thing they're probably going to teach you is meditation because meditation is about putting awareness on what is real and the only thing that is not real is what you think. It seems real, but it's not so, it is difficult to go from lower consciousness to higher consciousness because you have to get present to reality to start with and you have to learn to accept life as it is and ultimately learn surrender which is a non-doing. This runs counter to survival. This runs counter to our primal imperative to survive. Nowhere in our programming, genetically or causally, are we programmed to surrender. We're programmed to fight and resist and survive.

In going for higher consciousness, going for Enlightenment, we're actually going against our nature. We're going against our primal imperative to survive. This is why it is so difficult because we've developed default patterns of survival as well – default patterns of dreaming, default patterns of not being present here to reality. These things need to be looked at and changed. If we practise acceptance, we're starting to move to change because we're learning surrender. If we practise openness, same thing. If we practise meditation, we're recovering ourselves from a dream that we're lost in back to a form of reality, which is out here. There's nothing real about what's in your head. It's asleep. It's dreaming.

It is particularly difficult for people who've been programmed to be victims of life to raise their consciousness levels. People who constantly see themselves as victims of situations or other people or even themselves are in a bad dream. It's not real. You have to volunteer to be a victim. Bad stuff can happen, but you have to volunteer to be a victim of it. The moment you go into victim-orientated thinking, you've gone into lower consciousness and you've gone into dream.

The lowest part of that, of course, is anger. Anger is just a dream. Without dream, anger doesn't exist. When you blame something – yourself, a situation or another person – you get to be a victim.

To raise our consciousness levels, we need to learn to allay our nature, to learn to be present to reality. We need to practise openness and acceptance. There are some beautiful side effects of that. When we practise acceptance and openness, we start to find love. So that's very sweet.

If all we do in the world is practise closure and defensiveness, we cut ourselves off from the perception of love, and love is the true jewel of consciousness. In going for higher consciousness, people start perceiving love because they're opening up, they're dropping their defences. They're removing the obstacles that are in the way of higher consciousness and removing the obstacles that are in the way of Enlightenment.

It's really up to you. You're the only one who can change you. No one can do it for you. Someone can point it out for you, but only you can change you.

Any questions, any statements, any challenges to this teaching today?

S: Why are we born in lower consciousness when our true nature is pure consciousness?

V: Well, our true nature might be pure Beingness, it might be the ultimate, but our human nature is survival. And as such, it is lower consciousness, so we are born into lower consciousness because our awareness is on the animal, it's on the mind, it's on the body. And there's an identification with the mind and body which is a false identification, but it's there in humans. When awareness discovers itself – in other words, when you discover who you truly are – this identification drops because it's obviously not real. It's obviously false. But until then, it's a bit difficult. All you can do is work towards higher consciousness and the practices are simple. Practise openness, practise non-resistance, practise meditation, practise self-inquiry. Remove all of the beliefs that create you as a victim, because you're not: you have to volunteer to be a victim. Have a look and see for yourself.

S: Are some people more naturally awake than others so it's not as difficult in their practice to be with what's real?

V: Yes, that's because they've done it before. A lot of people don't remember past lives so they don't believe that past lives exist, but in my experience we've all lived before and we've all done this before. If we're interested in Truth, the chances are we've done it before many times, so whatever consciousness levels we managed to raise to in previous lives, we get that start in this life as well to some degree. It comes in seed form and it comes out. So yeah, some people come in more switched on, more alert and higher in consciousness than other people. That's true. Now we think, well, that's not fair, but of course it's fair. Everything's karmic. Everything's karmic. If you want to develop good karma you become a loving, caring, generous person. That's how it works really well. You want to develop negative karma? Just practise selfishness. It works the same way, except in the negative way. We create our own reality with the way we think. We are 100 per cent responsible.

~

S: I've read Osho saying that being a witness comes after long efforts of yoga because it's rare for someone only to be aware and succeed. He said that was his problem and it was a mistake for Krishnamurti to say to people "Just being aware is enough". Please can you comment?

V: Osho loved to have shots at Krishnamurti, let's put it that way. Osho's main methodology towards Enlightenment was witnessing, to watch the mind, to just keep witnessing the mind, develop that separation from the mind, detachment from the mind and just keep witnessing. At some point, you find yourself as the witness, you find yourself as pure awareness that is just aware of the mind.

At this point, you've woken up. You're no longer identified with the mind. It's gone. You're living as Beingness now. His methodology was witnessing. He talked about it over and over again. When he says that Krishnamurti's teaching wasn't enough, just to witness, well, that's debatable. Witnessing works. So does self-inquiry. So does meditation, and if you're really interested in Heart, openness works.

Non-resistance works – taking down all of the defence systems that are in the way of the perception of love. There are a few things that work. You've got to remember that Osho was a stirrer, and he loved to stir up other teachers. If you look at him from that angle, rather than what he's saying is absolutely factual on every occasion, you're going to see what a great sense of humour he really had.

~

S: When there are difficult things to express within a relationship, is the first step to accept the situation as it is?'

V: The first step is to accept the other. You know, when we have difficult times in relationships, we quite often take our own side, and in that way it becomes a bit of a war. If you really want good communication with anybody, make sure that you're not only on your own side, you're also on their side. And if you're on their side, you'll be able to put yourself in their shoes and you'll be able to hear them from their point of view, which actually facilitates communication.

Acceptance plays a big role in it, there's no doubt about it, but so does communication. When we truly look at what keeps relationships going in a healthy way, first communication, second commitment – those two things: commitment and communication. But when we're only taking our own side, inside a disagreement, in an argument, we've basically gone to war, and unfortunately the first casualty of war is usually truth. And this appears in the form of omission. Things aren't said that should be said. Things aren't owned, that should be owned. And so you have a look. Acceptance is great. Accepting the other is wonderful. Accepting everything as it is is wonderful, but if you want relationships to work well, particularly if you're in disagreements, make sure that you're on both sides: your side and their side.

~

S: Why do you think Osho was such a stirrer?

V: Because he was awake. People project onto awakened people all sorts of different things, but I've got to tell you right now you cannot control someone who's awake in any way. They are free. They're free to do whatever they want and someone who's awake who is teaching has set themselves up basically as a motivator. Someone who's awake holds a presence, and in that presence, you can find yourself as Truth. But in the meantime, what they do most of the time in satang is talk. The talks are motivators to get people to become willing enough to do whatever it takes to raise their consciousness levels and get free. Enlightenment. You listen to the different teachers and they're all in some way pointing to the Truth and trying to motivate people to do what's necessary to find themselves as Truth.

Osho was a great salesman for Truth, but he was a shit-stirrer. He just loved causing trouble. I remember a story that I heard about him when he was in university still studying how he would wear wooden shoes or wooden clogs along the corridors and the balconies on the wooden floor to make as much noise as possible to stir up as many people as possible. This was his nature. He was a stirrer. He liked to cause trouble. You see, look at it this way: if everybody's sleeping, and they are, how do you wake them up? Really, how do you wake them up? Do you think whispering sweet nothings in their ear and telling them how wonderful they are is going to work? I don't think so. You cause as much chaos as you can and then there might be a glimmer of awakening.

So Osho was a great stirrer. He caused all sorts of different devices to go off inside his own community and in the world in general. A device set by a master offers the potential of learning surrender and he was great at it. Nobody's ever really challenged sexuality the way he did. "From Sex to Superconsciousness". Everyone just bought it. There wouldn't be a harder way to get to superconsciousness than through sex. There wouldn't be a harder way. But what it does do, if you get involved in sex and you get involved in sleeping around, you get so many opportunities to surrender, to practise acceptance of life, because you cause so much trouble. It is a great big device. He would say "Well, why just have Italian? Why not have English food and Chinese food? Greek food? Why be stuck with one type of woman when you can have all this smorgasbord?"

What trouble that would cause and did. When you start playing with the primal imperatives of people, you're playing with something that can create an environment for surrender, an environment for acceptance, an environment to teach the mind exactly what it needs to learn to support higher consciousness and Enlightenment. All teachers teach surrender because it is the bottom line. It is the doorway. The Buddha sat under the Bodhi tree and surrendered, which means he did nothing – surrender is a non-doing – and he woke up. The practice of acceptance creates an environment of surrender. The harder life is, the more opportunities you have to practise surrender. Osho was a shit-stirrer and he was a master. He was a master at setting devices for thousands of people. Have a close look and see. Do you think he was really interested in sex? He'd gone way beyond.

~

S: Is it possible that you can have higher consciousness without knowing it, because that is how you were born?
V: Yeah, it's absolutely possible. Kids who are born with higher consciousness tend to be a challenge to their parents, to their peers and to their teachers because they know things. They see things that most don't. Quite often, they have the bigger picture in mind. Usually they're problem makers, and what era they are born in governs how they're treated.

I think it's probably a hard life where a child is born with higher consciousness because they're not likely to comply like other children. Someone with higher consciousness is not into compliance.

~

S: Since the time I started meditating regularly, I have found a lot of things I do meaningless. I used to enjoy what I was doing at work, but over time I feel it's meaningless and I question why I am here and what I am doing. Can you please comment?
V: Yeah. Look, since I've been a boy, I've been looking for the meaning of life and I have not been successful yet in finding one, and at some point, I got to see the pointlessness of it all – the pointlessness of just going to work to make money over and over every day. Same thing, repetitive, the same friends, the same conversations.

In looking for the meaning of life, I realised there probably isn't one, but what we can have is a beautiful life, and I found that to be true when I began serving Heart instead of serving myself. I'd served myself really well until I was 33 years old. I'd been successful in business, but even though I was financially okay, when I had a look at it, I found that I was broke because I didn't have much Heart, if any.

Being a businessman had closed me down too much and I started to realise that for 33 years, in a lot of ways, I'd wasted my life. It wasn't until I went into service of Heart that I felt that I was really living. I was getting what I call "manageable happiness" while in service to others, service to the plants, service to animals, service to anything besides me, and there was a certain joy that came, a certain happiness that came. I found that the way out of this sense of life being meaningless or pointless was to move into service, to move into a way of supporting love.

This is the Way of the Heart and you will discover that to serve Heart you have to be wide open. You have to drop all of your resistances, drop your defence systems, and walk through the world in a vulnerable way. This is the Beauty Way. This is the Way of the Heart. This is worthwhile.

~

S: I'm an Osho disciple. Everything that Osho, Ramana Maharshi, Mooji, Krishnamurti, Robert Adams, Adyashanti, Rupert Spira says resonates in my heart. When I look for "I", no "I" can be found. Everything is happening by itself. Perceiving is happening without a perceiver. The solid entity is absent, experiencing without the experiencer. But still the pull of desires is felt. Identification with the past happens itself in day-to-day life. Can you please comment?

V: It sounds like you're drifting from reality into dream and then back into reality because the truth is there is nobody here. There is a delusion that most humans have that there's somebody here and that's made up from memories of the past projecting to the future and a whole pile of belief systems they are identified with. When awareness starts to become aware of itself or when the witness starts to be known as self, that all disappears. People go through these different stages of slipping between that and flipping back to ego-based reality which is identification.

At this stage, self-inquiry is very helpful. When the mind comes back in with its thoughts about self, the question arises, "Who's aware? Who's aware of these thoughts?" In self-inquiry, the mind is actively attempting to turn the witness back to itself, to turn awareness back to itself. The flip-flopping can go on for a long time. For me, it went on for a whole year, flipping from Being-based reality to ego-based reality and back again. And in that year, there was a lot of self-inquiry. As a matter of fact, every thought that arose in the mind was challenged with the question "What's aware?" in an attempt to turn awareness back to itself, and it did.

It's easier if you're in the presence of someone who's awake, to do this to stay awake, particularly in the early stages, and I was very fortunate in the early years. There was another man in Perth, Western Australia, who was awake, called Devamarg. We used to spend a lot of time each day together, and we'd attend each other's satsangs and support each other in Truth. That was very helpful because I didn't have a sangha back then, I just had this one guy, and he had me.

After a while, it felt like awareness that was aware of itself had stuck to itself like two permanent magnets that couldn't be pulled apart, and the sense of identity completely disappeared. So that was like a death, a permanent death of the "I". It hasn't really arisen since. There's never a sense of anybody being here. Just nothing talking, that's it.

While you're at a stage of flip-flopping, flipping between ego-based reality and Being-based reality, keep supporting Truth. Don't support the ego. The mind is the one that does the support. Keep supporting Truth. It'll support meditation. It'll support self-inquiry. It'll support openness. Give your life to Truth and be free.

~

S: Since the last time I spoke to you, I'll be listening to you in my car on the way to work, and even now, I'm trying to remember this question that keeps coming and going and I'm battling to get it out, but it really does feel like for me at this stage of my life Vishrant... where I'm toggling between this massive expansiveness that seems to be wanting to pull me in and this terrible pain of still being me, this person... that it kind of bugs me when you say that it's up to you to do these things, you know, because I try. But it feels like the thing that's trying is getting weaker and weaker. So I don't know if I'm explaining myself well. It feels like something big wants to pull even the trying away. When I talk to you, I feel this going away as well. Anyway, it's not really a question.

V: I do have a comment on it. It's like somewhere, there's not an acceptance of the one that's trying. Somewhere there's resistance and that resistance itself keeps bringing that somebody back. Everything has to be accepted, including the loss of Beingness. Everything has to be accepted, and in that the mind can then rest. It can never rest while it's in resistance to anything.

S: Right so it just feels like a conundrum. It just feels like this.

V: Then you make a conundrum okay.

S: Okay. All right, so just accept . . . just accept the pain and the frustration and just watch it?

V: Yes, that is the answer. The answer is relaxing. That's actually why I was given the name Vishrant because I wasn't relaxed as a businessman when I applied for sannyas. My name that was given to me actually means "relax" because it's what I needed to learn.

S: Yeah, thank you very much. I really appreciate that. It's like my whole heart just wants to jump out and I just want to expand and yet there's just this tiny little niggly voice in the back going "No, you've got to try harder. You've got to do your work."

V: The want is the problem. The wanting, the want itself is resistance.

S: Yes, but you said the one desire that's worth keeping is the one that wants freedom, wants Truth, and now that is there, I know it's there. Otherwise, this wouldn't keep happening every day when I wake up. It comes back, you know. It's there all the time.

V: You're very difficult to teach. That last want has to die, but it doesn't die until the end. The desire for freedom, the desire for Enlightenment has to be there, but towards the end it has to die too and it sounds like it's possible it's near the end for you. So that want also has to die.

S: Thank you. Thank you very much for your time Vishrant.

V: The ego hangs out and survives through all sorts of methodologies towards the end. Mostly it creates helper thoughts to help you become enlightened, but they are also in the way because that's just the ego trying to survive. And it needs to learn to lie down. It needs to learn to surrender. All desires are in the way. All attachments are in the way. Let everything go.

~

S: Can you describe "one consciousness" and how to practice and realise that? Are there any specific exercises you can suggest?

V: Okay, so you can't really practise one consciousness because one consciousness is what is. It's the Truth, but human beings have created themselves as separate by having a mind that sees itself as separate. You take away the mind and there is no separation. We are one. It is the mind, particularly the ego which is the identified mind, that creates itself as separate.

You surrender that, and you find you are one. Particularly if you find yourself as Beingness, you're just everything, you can't be separate.

There is no duality then. The only time duality comes into play is when someone's ego-based, they think they're a somebody, and they think they're looking for God. That's God looking for God. There is no genuine separation, only an illusion of separation caused by the identified part of the mind thinking that somehow it's separate and there's somewhere to go. There's nowhere to go. You already are Beingness. You already are oneness. The only thing that's in the way is the "I".

Let go, let go, let go and turn awareness onto itself. Turn that that's aware of the mind back to itself. The whole thing with oneness? People look for oneness. We already are that. You're looking for something you already are. You just do not perceive it because you perceive it through the vehicle of the "I", through the mind which is not even real. Let go. Let go. Let go.

~

S: Thank you so much for answering and having these calls, I literally just found you.

There's something way beyond me working here, that's for sure. I also have a little bit of what the last person was talking about. So there are times when it's like coming out of a deep meditation when I can stay in that space for maybe a few hours. Then towards the latter part of the day it kind of gets back to "Okay, now what?" It just gets back to the person, and I don't want to call it an excruciating pain, but it seems like that. The wanting to experience the oneness which we are, I understand that, but somehow, it's not happening, so that's why I was asking because I was listening to some of the Upanishads and there are some practices like the om practice where you just drop all of those states and differences. So I was just curious if you had anything like that or is it just surrender every single time? Also, when you talk about desires, I mean I assume you're not talking about coffee and you know clothes and things or are you?

V: Anything that creates resistance brings awareness to the mind to some degree and when a person is first starting to find Beingness itself or an emptiness or a oneness of all, awareness tends to go back to the mind if the mind's contracting, so creating a mind that doesn't create resistance is a really good idea. In Buddhism, it's called an equanimous mind – a mind that basically stays pretty level with whatever's happening, a mind that can take fire without reacting, and that's very difficult for us as human beings because we're so defended, but we can do it, we can learn to let go.

We can learn and train the mind to let go and be at peace and so people wake up and they stay awake, but that's probably because their mind is supporting that somewhere. A mind that is willing to let go, a mind that is willing to self-inquire, this is the right way to go.

I followed the Way of the Heart which absolutely annihilated my ego. The Way of the Heart dictates that you be in service to others, you be in service to the planet, you be in service to animals and plants. Whatever you're doing, you be in service, and in that, if you're genuinely doing that, you become very humbled. And humility is basically an absence of the "I". True humility is an absence of the "I". And so for me there were two wings happening. One was the wing of discipline which was self-inquiry and meditation. The other was the wing of the Heart which was practised through openness, generosity, kindness, giving. Two wings to fly with in the marketplace.

So I kind of teach that methodology, the Way of the Heart combined with discipline, combined with meditation, self-inquiry, whatever else, yoga, whatever works basically. I'm not particular on anything. If it works, it's a good way to go.

As far as the mind coming back and the pain of that coming back, you have to accept that there's a karmic number going on as well and that we actually have to pay back our debts whatever they might be, and karma plays a role in Enlightenment. Two people can do exactly the same things to prepare for Enlightenment. One can wake up and one may not wake up. There's a karmic element in it and you've got to accept karma. You've got to accept that, well, this is what is. In the acceptance you can find peace. In non-acceptance – which is resistance – you can't find peace, and as a matter of fact you're getting in the way of Enlightenment because you're creating contraction.

S: Yeah, that makes sense.

V: It's really about accepting life as it is. In a way, becoming a fatalist, you know, because karma is gonna take you out or it's gonna put you in. We have to pay our bills back. We can't get away with anything, and so whatever merit we have, we get that, and whatever detriment, we get that.

In Buddhism, you go into a monastery and you talk to one of the ajahns and ask, "Oh, how can I raise my consciousness levels?" And they'll say, well, you can become a monk or a nun, and you may say, "No, I don't want to do that, I want to be a lay person". And they'll say, well, become generous, become giving, become a kind person, and they're right. They're absolutely right because you accrue beautiful karma and you also have a nice life. So I advocate the Way of the Heart and discipline: both wings to fly with in the marketplace.
S: Okay.
V: Where are you, what country?
S: I'm located in New York so I just happened to run across your live broadcast.
V: Yeah, you guys in New York, you guys are vaccinating pretty quickly over there.
S: I have got one shot. I have one more to go which comes in two weeks, but you still have to be careful because the way the vaccines work is that you cannot get it, but you can actually give it. You have to wear your mask and do other things, but you won't get sick from it.
V: Yeah right, yeah, I understand what you're saying, yeah. Well, I wish you the very, very best there.

We're fortunate here in Western Australia where there isn't any virus at the moment. We're actually virus-free and we're vaccinating, the people are being vaccinated slowly, very slowly, but we're free, so watching the news and finding out what's happened in America and what's been happening in America, it's heartbreaking.

S: Yeah, it is, and you know I kind of have this double view about that which is which side of the coin is it? I mean, is it nature telling us we're not accepting and doing, and even after all of the heartbreaks and all of the news and all of the doctors telling people to wear masks and be careful, they don't do it. So then you say, well okay, what can I do? If I have to be out then I wear a double mask. If not, I stay inside and I find you. That's pretty amazing to me.

V: I went into not knowing 22 years ago because when we try to know anything we get locked in our minds, and the reason we want to know is because we want to survive. It's a survival mechanism. But when we go to "I don't know," there's no story anymore. It's over, and our mind starts to quieten down. I've been in "I don't know" for about 22 years. It's lovely. It's like being a little kid again in wonderment.

S: You know it's quite remarkable. My ego would say "Oh I'm an intellectual. I have to have an answer for everything. I'm a scientist" and that alone gets in the way.

V: It does. And look, I have a mind that's reasonably good at mechanics and working out things as well. I just love "I don't know".

S: Yeah okay, I think I will adopt that as a mantra from now going on, going forward.

V: Really, it's a sweet one because it means you're not living in your head trying to problem-solve constantly. You're actually okay with not knowing.

S: I have to say I've come a long way since I started because if it wasn't an equation, I wasn't interested. I've come quite a long way, so it's just the continuation of that practice and I think I will remember what you just said and use it as a mantra and just remember that's where it's all at.

V: What it'll give you is freedom, freedom from this *pointing at his head* because this is the prison. The mind is the prison.

S: Yeah, yes, I recognize that.

V: Nice talking to you.

S: Thank you so much.

~

S: When I am peaceful, I still ask myself, "Is that all? Is it that easy?" I feel I must do something. Why is that so?

V: You have a mind that is trying to help you and that's what it's been programmed to do, to help you, and it's now in the way. It was trying to help when it should have been resting, but that's how you've been programmed. You've been programmed to develop a mind that looks for problems and solve them and this is the case for everybody who's been to school. We've been programmed to look for problems and solve them, and of course this is not actually restful, it is not relaxing, it is work, but it's how we're programmed.

For me to learn not to do that was quite difficult. I was just talking about "I don't know" – a beautiful answer to everything. In truth, most of the time we don't know, we're just guessing, but we're keeping ourselves locked in our mind trying to work it out, trying to analyse, trying to problem solve. We didn't go to school and get taught how to be happy. We went to school and we were taught how to be efficient little problem solvers. For most human beings, they stay efficient little problem solvers until they die, but we can reverse that. We can reverse engineer it and go back to what we were like when we were little kids, which is being here in no-mind, in wonderment, in not knowing.

It's up to you. You're going to create your reality by the way you think.

~

S: I can feel now that I've been looking to get ahead in life and protecting the Heart. Now that I stopped this, there is a pronounced feeling of a very vulnerable heart that is in front of everything. Is this what you mean by openness?

V: Yes. Yes, in the beginning it feels vulnerable because it's been defended for so long that you notice the change, you notice the vulnerability. After a while of being wide open, you don't notice. The vulnerability becomes ordinary. It's only when you're first opening up that you notice that you're vulnerable because you're not used to it. It's not normal for you. You're used to hiding behind something, some kind of defence system, and the Way of the Heart dictates that you walk through the world undefended, vulnerable. But after a while it just becomes ordinary. You don't notice that you're vulnerable. You're just open, and it's beautiful because you love. You perceive love, love everything and everybody, love the good, the bad and the ugly. The Way of the Heart is a beautiful way to live as a human being.

~

S: I've been doing self-inquiry for three years, spending many hours on it. Not sure when I'll be awake, feeling very helpless, even trying to see who is feeling helpless and tired. When I do self-inquiry, a lot of energy movement is observed between the chest that is circulating and causing pain. It feels like some energy is blocked. This all started happening since I did vipassana. This desire to be free is always on the mind. It's not dropping. It seems that the mind is not stopping its efforts. Can you please comment?

V: Human beings tend to be full of pain. They carry pain bodies or repressed emotions or traumas, and as you start getting free, as you start opening up, all of these traumas, all of this pain, this unfinished business starts coming to the surface so it can be freed – and people aren't expecting that. They're expecting light, expecting love, they're expecting openness, but really there's a certain amount of laundry that's required to clean – whatever has been repressed over lifetimes.

When you start opening up, you find that all sorts of things start moving around in you. Different energy fields in the body start opening up, particularly if you're doing yoga or qigong or tai chi. These methodologies also help open the body further and release what's inside, but what's required more than anything else is the willingness to be okay with whatever appears. If discomfort appears, the willingness to be okay with it, the willingness to be warmly okay with it is best. Then it can leave and you can be free of that guest of yours you've had for a long time.

This is another reason why it's so difficult to go from lower consciousness to higher consciousness, because when a person starts doing the work on themselves to open themselves up, all of these unfinished businesses, all of these pain bodies, all of this trauma that may be caught inside starts to surface and wants to come out, and it feels pretty awful. There's hopelessness and helplessness in it, not just pain, and so people try to avoid it, but that's what they've been doing their whole lives. That's why it's locked in there.

When we are genuinely warmly welcoming to whatever appears inside of us, we are really healing our psyches. We're really emptying the pain body out. We're preparing ourselves for higher consciousness. We're preparing ourselves for Enlightenment. Let everything be okay. Let everything be okay. It doesn't matter how uncomfortable it is, just make it okay. It's better out than in, always.

~

S: How about when developmental trauma is on board? It feels impossible yet necessary. I watched one of your videos about being in the marketplace with stuck energy.

V: Well, I had to deal with that. I actually had a very rough upbringing as a child, institutionalised in a Catholic boarding school and basically tormented for eight years. I had a lot of trauma by the time I left school. I was a very closed, very angry young man, and I had to find a way to deal with it, and I did because my main defence system was anger and anger is just violence. I got to examine anger. It's a defence system that stops us from feeling something that's been touched. I decided that what I'd do was instead of defending myself from feeling, I would start to allow myself to feel. I wouldn't encourage anger, I wouldn't support anger, because with anger, you've got to be a victim, you've got to be blaming someone or something or yourself.

I stopped blaming and I started owning, and made owning the touch – whatever someone did or said that touched me or touched probably trauma – I would go okay, that's okay, and I'd allow myself to feel the touch. In the feeling, I started to heal the wounding, and over years, it all got healed because of that willingness – instead of reacting and defending, to allow it to be touched, to allow myself to feel the wounding, which quite often had helplessness and hopelessness in it. But I wasn't interested in being wounded. And I wasn't interested in being controlled by the fear of feeling my wounding so I decided to heal it all. Anytime I got touched, anytime someone or something happened that touched me, instead of contracting and protecting myself, I'd allow myself to feel. I'd allow myself to be with what had been touched and I started to heal. My understanding is clearly that we heal our wounding by feeling it. It's been locked into our bodies. It's a prisoner. It wants to get free because it's compressed energy. In our willingness to feel, we can start to heal. And I'm never ever going to suggest to anybody that that's easy. It's hard. But if you don't give yourself a choice – which is what discipline is – you can do it. It's up to you.

~

S: I'm just following up on something you said earlier about finding someone who's already aware to help you. Does it have to be somebody in person? Because of the pandemic situation, it's almost impossible to go somewhere physically. How do you do this given what's going on in the world?

V: Yeah. So I may have made a mistake, but you may have heard me wrong. Find someone awake. Find someone who's awake, someone who's enlightened. I was very fortunate in my life that I had Osho Rajneesh as my teacher for eight years and he was awake. Then when the Advaita Vedanta teachers started coming to Perth, I would go to all of their retreats, go to all of their meetings, all of their satsangs. I was able to sit in the presence of people who were awake. I started hosting the Advaita Vedanta teachers in Perth, Western Australia. They'd come stay in my house and I got to be very close. That proximity definitely helps because anyone who's awake carries an energy field, a Buddha field. In that Buddha field, it is so much easier to surrender. It is so much easier to find awareness itself and what I've found in doing satsang online with people all around the world is people are falling in once they learn to tune in because the energy field seems to be transmitted through the Internet. I have no idea how, but I have people having satoris all over the world simply by coming to satsang like you are right now and tuning into the energy field.

S: Thank you.

V: You're very welcome. Just let go. Let go. Let go.

Thank you for satsang. Good to see you bravehearts here today.

CHAPTER TWELVE

Why Saying Yes Works

V: If we have a look at the opposite to saying Yes which is No, and No is a form of resistance, and if we are able to look at our minds with clarity, we can see that all forms of resistance create a level of dissatisfaction or a level of suffering.

So in learning to have a Yes to life, and acceptance of life as it is, we start to eliminate suffering. We start to eliminate the possibility of unconsciousness. In Yes, we can stay clear. We can have clarity. In No, when we go into resistance, usually there's a story with that resistance, possibly victim-oriented. In the story or the drama, we're actually going into lower consciousness because we're dreaming.

In Yes, there's no real dream. It's just okay. What is is what is. Our consciousness levels can actually rise in a Yes, whereas they don't rise in a No or in resistance because of the dream element that's attached to it. It comes back to the question: how conscious do you want to be? And how much do you really want to suffer? If we resist life, we create suffering for ourselves, and it may not change much. But if we're okay with life, we don't suffer. We can still move to change from that okayness if we want to – we can still move to change from openness if we want to because Yes is a very open way of living and No is a very closed way of living.

Primarily, we're programmed to resist life. We're programmed to survive, and in a lot of ways the No supports that. The No supports the resistance because it helps us survive, but if we're going for higher consciousness, it's actually in the opposite direction. It's the opposite way. If we find a Yes, our consciousness levels start to rise because first of all we're just leaving dream behind and we're leaving some level of dissatisfaction or suffering behind as well. Yes is the Way of the Heart because non-resistance is the Way of the Heart.

Tosh: Hello Vishrant, you're muted at the moment.
V: Hello, it looks like we just went off here for a little bit, something to do with a technical difficulty. Such is life. So yeah, I could have gone into resistance then because we lost power or we lost something, we lost activity on the Internet, but what's the point? Why not just accept that this is what it is and leave it at that? Why go into resistance? Why create stress? Why create suffering? There's no need. It's actually okay as it is. Everything's okay.

As I was saying, we can resist life, we can go "Oh that shouldn't be happening" and go into internal resistance or we can accept life as it is and be okay, and not suffer. Negative things happen. It's just the world we live in. It's the way it is, and we can either resist those things or we can accept those things. People think if we accept, we don't move to change, we don't move to alter things, but that's not true. From a place of non-resistance, from a place of openness, we can change everything. We can just do it from a cool place that is switched on.

The key to higher consciousness, the key to Enlightenment and the key to the Way of the Heart is acceptance of life as it is rather than resistance to life as it is. This Yes that I talk about sometimes is important because it helps us be free of suffering. It helps us raise our consciousness levels. It helps us find and perceive Heart.

Ultimately, unconditional surrender is supported by Yes and unconditional surrender seems to be a requirement for Enlightenment, from the perspective of the mind. It's up to you. You're the one who's going to create your reality because you're the one who's in charge of your thinking. Nobody's doing it to you. You're the one who's applying a Yes or No to life. You're the one who's either resisting or not resisting, so you can't blame anyone else. You are 100 per cent responsible for your reality. Life is the way it is. Sometimes things work out the way you want and sometimes they don't. If we can be okay, if we can have a Yes to both, life's a breeze.

S: Hello Vishrant, how are you?

V: Blissed out to the max.

S: That's such a habitual question. I knew I wouldn't get an ordinary response from you.

So I am only, 20 but I feel like I've been on this path since I was about 16, but very seriously since 18. Since then, I have felt very old in my body and my body has experienced a lot of pain as well. Funnily enough, I feel like I'm 60 in this body sometimes.

Last year, I maybe had what some call a spiritual awakening, where for four months I felt like I was in hell, but I knew that it was necessary for my growth.

I was meditating five hours a day. I was constantly fatigued. I didn't know what I wanted to do with my future. I'm studying science and one day I got up and just left my biology exam thinking, that's it, I'm going to Croatia and I'm going to live with a guru in a spiritual community because I'd watched a video of this guru a few nights before that. Then I got home and my mum reacted like I'd been shot, you know, by a bullet. I saw some people who work with energy and I started to feel more like myself again.

As I reflect on that there was definitely a dissolving of self, but it wasn't so pretty. A lot of things have happened after that period. I was the most joyous I've ever been. I met a girlfriend and she was the first, she's my first girlfriend. It's quite a deep love connection and she's also very deep and spiritual in her own way. But now I feel like again this thing is coming over me, but it's definitely different to the last time. I feel more silence. I do feel more grounded, but as this presence comes into me, there's also – and this is getting to my question – there's also this feeling of boredom, although my suffering seems to have decreased, or at least there seems to be a bit more ease in my life. This feeling of egolessness, or at least I wouldn't say I'm totally there, seems to be dissolving in some ways leaving me with this feeling of emptiness almost. I'm sure it may pass, but that's kind of where I'm currently at and I was just wondering about your thoughts on that.

V: You've made a lot of statements there and some of it rings true to what happened to me. I became a seeker when I was very young. I was interested in it when I was probably 12 and continued on from there. I went on to become a businessman instead of taking a spiritual life and I ended up giving that business life up for a spiritual life, simply because of the calling which sounds like you have. The seeker in you is just wanting to come home and has had a bit of a taste of it and you want some more and it will haunt you unless you serve it as it haunted me until I served it.

As Westerners, we don't tend to think there's such a thing as past lives, but I can tell you right now there are, and if you've got a calling, more than likely you've done this a lot of times before and it's calling you home. If you don't follow it, I think you'll have regrets. I've been with the gurus. I went and hung out with the gurus, with the awakened ones, because in their energy field I could find myself as Truth. Eventually, I could find myself as Truth when they weren't there, but it was because of their energy fields that I allowed myself to die in, to say Yes in, to just give everything away in, that I found that I was everything. You sound like a seeker, and look, once you've begun the journey, it's best to complete it, you know?

S: Yeah. Yeah.
V: So you went to Croatia? Where are you now?
S: I'm in Melbourne and actually I've just started seeing someone that you might know, Sailor Bob Adamson?
V: Yeah, I know Sailor Bob.

S: I found you because of Osho. There's just this deep resonance with Osho that I could not explain. I originally watched the Wild Wild Country documentary that painted this dim picture around him. Then when one of my mates just said, "Oh you should listen to this guy," Osho, and I listened to him and it blew my mind. Then I read about five or six of his books and he was really instrumental in opening up my Heart as well, just the way he talks about love was just incredible. It's funny, because I had the feeling that Osho as a guru hadn't enlightened anyone and then I found that interview that you did with him a day later and I saw that there's the Vishrant Buddhist Society and I clicked on the channel. When I start watching your videos and your story and that you're Australian, it hit home a little bit as well.

I'm in Melbourne. I didn't actually end up going to Croatia. I wanted to, but I am still studying. So yeah, I'm in Melbourne at the moment.

V: You have a calling. You've been called to wake up. Now it's up to you. Now it's up to you and you've got all of these distractions in front of you. Everybody who's a seeker does. We get the distractions of sexuality and distractions of relationship, distractions of needing to be successful, to prove ourselves to the world, the distraction of needing to get a degree because we think that's going to make us successful and happy. All of these distractions get presented to you, there's no doubt about that, but the calling is there mate. Follow your Heart. That's my advice. Follow your Heart because your Heart actually knows which way to go. But when you're listening to your Heart, it doesn't talk in words. It just knows which way to go. I followed my path and that cost me my relationship because my fiancé didn't want to get involved in spirituality. It cost me my businesses – which were multimillion dollar businesses – because they were in the way, so I gave them up as well, because I followed my Heart and I found myself as Truth.

S: Thank you Vishrant.

~

S: Vishrant, what can help me say No less and less? Love from Peru.

V: Who's in charge of the No? Who's in charge of saying No? You've got to own up. It's you. You're in charge of saying No. So if you're in charge of saying No, you're also in charge of saying Yes. Choose Yes because it's a choice. Choose Yes. Choose acceptance instead of resistance. You choose your choice.

~

S: Sometimes when we're forced into something, there's resistance in Yes. What do you suggest here?

V: That's not the type of Yes I'm talking about. You see, if there's a resistance in Yes. then there's some form of non-acceptance in the Yes. A true Yes has acceptance in it and there is no resistance in it. If there's resistance in the Yes, it's actually a No. It's a No pretending to be a Yes. A true Yes has acceptance in it and there is no resistance.

~

S: Does a person's maturity level impact their ability to have a Yes to life?

V: Yes, it does. Immature people live in a No quite a lot. They resist life. They turn themselves into victims of this and that, and they take offence to things all over the place, offer resistance and suffer incredibly. Immaturity is something that's really not worth having. The best thing as a human being you can do is develop maturity, and quite often the way to do this is to watch other people who are mature and role model off them. Copy them and then copy them long enough until it becomes your own default patterning. It is quite possible that we didn't grow up in an environment that offered maturity. Maybe our parents weren't mature. Maybe our teachers weren't mature. Maybe our peers weren't mature, but that's no reason why you can't develop maturity. Find people who are mature, who are living mature lives. Watch them and copy them until it becomes your own default pattern because to be immature in this world is a handicap not an advantage. Immature people suffer incredibly at their own hand and usually they try to include other people in their suffering. Mature adults don't do that.

~

S: How can one tune in with you in online satsangs?
V: Find a big Yes and tune into the energy field. There's an energy field here. Tune into it. You might find it start to expand your mind a little bit, maybe a bit of pressure around the crown, maybe a little bit in the third eye. The transmission is happening. Open up and feel it.

S: How does having a Yes impact the relationship between a student and spiritual teacher?

V: There is no other way to be with a spiritual teacher, but with a Yes because the spiritual teacher is going to take you into the unknown and usually when we meet the unknown, we develop some form of No. Unfortunately, that doesn't work. That keeps you stuck in lower consciousness. The spiritual teacher is trying to take you beyond the mind into the unknown, into Beingness.

The mind needs to have a Yes to play that game. It's your willingness that allows things to occur. If you develop a No or you develop resistance, well, you're not going to go anywhere. You're going to stay stuck where you are. You will stay stuck in lower consciousness. It is a Yes that can set you free, not a No. It is unconditional surrender ultimately that will support Enlightenment, and the only way you can get there is through acceptance. You can't get there through resistance. Resistance might be really good in the marketplace if you're trying to build a business or you're at the gym trying to build muscles, but in the game of higher consciousness it does not work. What works is acceptance and surrender and that's a Yes.

~

S: Hello Vishrant, is it necessary for someone to teach when Enlightenment happens? Like in the case of the Buddha, many people came to him and requested him to teach spirituality.

V: Yeah, that's what happened here too. People started noticing the energy field and they started wanting to come and sit with me because the energy field itself advertises itself. Those who are sensitive enough to perceive it know what it means. They know that someone's awake because the energy field or the Buddha field, if it's continuous, is the only way to tell if someone's awake.

Different teachers have different personalities and different ways of being in the world. They're not the same. You can't tell if someone's awake simply by what they say because everything that an awakened teacher says can be found in a library somewhere. It's been around for a long time. The only way to see if someone is awake is to perceive the energy field around them. This is why people started coming. They started to perceive the energy field, a Buddha field. They started to find peace in it, their minds started expanding, started disappearing, because that's what happens in a Buddha field, their hearts started opening. So you find someone who has this permanent Buddha field and you've found someone who's awake. It's the only way to tell if they're awake. It doesn't necessarily matter what they're saying or doing. The Buddha field says at all. It can't lie.

~

S: What is your opinion of hanging around people who cause me to have resistance?
V: Perfect opportunities for learning surrender. You see I think that I learned more from my wife about surrender than I did from anything else. My wife and I were very different people. We had different opinions about things. We didn't see eye to eye quite often but that gave me the opportunity to practice acceptance and surrender. In hanging out or hanging around with

someone who was actually possibly causing resistance in me, I learned to die. I learned to surrender unconditionally. For those of us in the marketplace who hold down jobs and have families, every time we find ourselves in resistance, we can use that to practice acceptance, and surrender. This is a spiritual practice that takes you home if you want but most people tend to practice resistance and suffer. You don't need to. Find a way to accept what is happening. Find a way to be open. Find a way to stay equanimous. It's up to you, up to you.

~

S: Hello Vishrant, namaste. Why does it take so much time for Enlightenment to happen, the years of practice required?

V: It takes more than one lifetime. See, people seem to think that this is the only life that we have and this is the only time that we've put effort into trying to wake up. My memory tells me that I've done this for hundreds of lifetimes. I look at people who are awake who have woken up easily and I know they have done the work – maybe not this lifetime, but previous lifetimes. We look at people who wake up at birth or wake up at a very young age like Amma, she's done it before. It's not just this lifetime, and it does take a long time.

It takes an awful long time unless you become very willing, unless you become willing to give yourself to Truth instead of giving yourself to yourself. Instead of serving you, you start serving Truth, and when the mind starts serving Truth, awareness can stay on

Truth. Enlightenment can happen. But it takes a fair bit to get to that stage. It takes a fair bit of consciousness to get to a stage where you realise that resistance, every bit of resistance you offer, is you creating suffering for yourself. It takes a fair bit of work. The highway or the freeway to waking up is to hang out with someone who's awake because they'll teach you how to surrender. They'll teach you how to accept life. I mean, they don't have much else to teach you besides having a Buddha field that you can die in, that you can dissolve in, that you can disappear in. That's what they teach. They all teach the same thing: accept, let go, open up, and surrender. The very thing that goes against our survival mechanism is what is taught to take people to superconsciousness.

And yes, it takes time. Lifetimes. Whether you remember that or not doesn't matter. Put your totality into anything in life and you're likely to achieve it, including spirituality. See, a lot of people say, "Well, do you need to become a monk or a nun, enter a monastery or an ashram?" No, you can do it in the marketplace. You just have to put Truth first, and Heart first, and then your family, then your job and then whatever else – but Truth and Heart have to be first.

Whatever we put first is going to win. So we can be in the marketplace, we can have a family, raise our children. We can hold down a job, do the chores, and we can practise openness, we can practise acceptance, we can practise meditation and we can practise self-inquiry while in the marketplace. We can wake up here, now.

S: How does one know if the third eye has opened up?
V: See, that's a curiosity question from the ego which doesn't help people wake up. It's a trap. It entertains the mind in a way so it gets caught in opening the third eye and it becomes fascinated with that. You're better off being fascinated with opening the crown chakra. The crown chakra connects us with everything as everything. The third eye, when it opens, does give us access to the Akashic records. It gives us access to clear seeing, but the ego can use that for itself. When the crown opens and there's this connection with everything, the "I" starts to disappear because you lose touch with it. You find yourself as everything so there's no "I", there's no you, there's you as everything, and this is a satori.

So when you put your awareness on your crown you can experience satoris which are not really experiences, it's just the words I have to use: it's knowing self as everything. And if that stays 24 hours a day, seven days a week, if that stays, you're awake, because you're knowing yourself as Truth in that the "I" has dropped because it is seen for what it is, fraudulent. There's nothing real about the "I". It's totally imagined. There's nothing real at all about it.

It's like, here we are as Beingness, pure consciousness, pure awareness. Here we are as Beingness using a spacesuit that has an on-board computer to visit this realm, but people think they're the spacesuit. They think they're the on-board computer. We're this that's purely aware, using the spacesuit.

~

S: Can a Buddha or awakened being fully operate in the world and be an academic and engineer, a builder, etc.?

V: I really don't know. I had a fair bit of trouble operating in the world in the beginning because I just wanted to sit still all day long and stare at space. But now, 22 years on from awakening, I'm running a Buddhist society and a wellness centre with staff, so it's possible. It is difficult though because I don't live in my head so I need a lot of reminders as to what I need to be doing and when. But it's possible. It's just a different way of being in the world. Ego-based reality is really living in the head and operating from the head, the mind, and Being-based reality is operating from Beingness. It's very different. It's like if you got into my head you'd wonder where the hell I'd gone. There's no one there. There are no thoughts. My mind is silent. There's no editor, and that's very different because there's no safety, there's no safety in Beingness. The ego is constantly thinking about safety, protecting itself by editing what it says and checking out which way to go. Whereas in Beingness, first of all, there is no fear so it's a very different way of living, but it's possible. I don't know if you could work as an engineer. I just don't know.

~

S: Is keeping quiet and saying Yes the same thing?

V: No. You can definitely keep quiet in a No. It's called sulking. A Yes is a wide openness, and being in silence, you can also be wide open, but there can be a No in silence. How about just be wide open all the time, be vulnerable all of the time so the world can pass through you instead of getting caught in you? That's nice.

~

S: Is Enlightenment the end stage? Is this cycle of birth and rebirth finished?
V: I think the Truth is I don't know because I'm not dead. When I die, we'll see. I don't think there's anything here to come back, but I don't know. It's like I could say I know, but I don't. It's just now and this is real now and when I look for someone here now I can't find anybody. There's talking, but there's nobody talking so I don't think there's anything to come back, but I don't know. I've read all of the scriptures of the Buddha in the sutras, and I have an understanding from them as to what other masters have said, but I don't know. I don't take anything from a book and believe it ever. I put everything that is not my own direct experience in the "maybe" column because it's not safe to take on beliefs. They're prisons. You are better off to be a beginner always, not knowing always, and that way the universe can flow through you. You're not stuck. Those who think they know are actually lost. They're stuck.

~

S: Vishrant, what does openness mean?
V: Closed/open, defended/undefended, imprisoned/free: I hope that helps. When you open, nothing is contracted inside, everything is flat-lined like you're at a zero level. It's so nice. When you were a baby, you

were wide open, and then you learnt to close to protect yourself from all sorts of different things. That's normal, but as adults, because we're intelligent, we can learn to open up again. We can live open and vulnerable, and this openness, this vulnerability supports Enlightenment, supports higher consciousness and supports Heart, supports the beauty. Closure is very protective, very protective, and that's survival, but we're intelligent enough to go beyond that.

~

S: Hi, Vishrant do you find any value in astrology?
V: I like the now. I'm not interested in the future. I'm not interested in the past. I like the now – and I've liked the now most of my life that I can remember because the now is real. This constant need to understand, this constant need to know keeps us in a state of tension. Just be in love with the now and then you can truly live. As long as we're projecting forward and remembering back we're existing, but we are existing in a dream. We're not living. And so look, even if astrology does have favour in it, I have no interest in it. I don't want to know the future. I don't want to know anything about the future or anything about the past really, because they take away from this beautiful, pristine moment. As far as wanting to know about my character, all I have to do to know how that works is to witness the mind, to develop a silent witness and simply keep watching, and then the mind shows itself, shows everything, shows all of its aspects. So I don't really get into anything that involves the future, the past, can't be

bothered. There's so much beauty to live here now, to be here now, to be open now. It's not that I haven't been involved in astrology. Like most seekers, I got involved and I studied astrology. I must admit at the time it fascinated me, but when I really look at why, it was once again me trying to control my environment through understanding rather than just letting go and being. Let go and be. It's beautiful.

~

S: Do different masters bear different fruits? For instance, with you, my Heart is feeling very expanded. Is this because your path to Enlightenment was from the Heart?

V: I was with Osho, Bhagwan Shree Rajneesh as he was known, when I first came across him. He was a Heart teacher and I definitely did not have Heart. As a matter of fact, I consider that the first 33 years of my life were wasted because I didn't have Heart. The realisation that I didn't have Heart was the result of hanging out in his scene with his sannyasins. I decided to pursue Heart, find that beauty and live it. I gave my life to Heart before I gave my life to Truth.

I gave my life to Heart. From my perspective, that meant being in service because when we find love, we just want to help people. We just want to take care of people. That's how the mind works when it's affected by Heart. So yeah, I'm definitely into Heart because I had a Heart teacher. Osho was a Heart teacher and Heart is the pathway to superconsciousness and to Enlightenment because it's the same deal. You have to surrender. You have to put yourself aside and you have to accept life. It's the same way. I've been loving now for 34 years and that is so nice. Love is the true jewel of consciousness. It's the very thing that is lacking here on this planet. There's too much mind and not enough love. If there was just love, we'd have such a beautiful place here, but because there's so much mind, there's wars, there's terrorism, there's rapes, there's murders, there's theft, there's starvation – all of these negative things are brought about by a lack of Heart. Because when we love, when we perceive love, we just want to take care of everyone and everything. This is the Way of the Heart.

~

S: Why don't you identify with being an ego again? Then that way, you can come back for sure and help more people be awake.

V: It's pretty hard to identify with something you're not. That would be like me identifying with my clothes. How can I say my clothes are me? They're obviously my clothes. How can I say this body is me? How can I say this mind is me? It's obviously a costume. It's obviously an outfit, a spacesuit. Looking from the perspective of Beingness, how can this be me when I'm everything? Not possible. Try to identify with being an "I" again? That would be crazy. That really would be like me identifying with being my clothes. Well, maybe identifying with being a mouse. You see, the thing about waking up is the identity drops. It can't possibly be real anymore because it's seen for what it is, absolutely fraudulent. We are Beingness. We are pure consciousness, pure awareness. That's what we are and when that is known, when it knows itself, when awareness locks onto itself, it's not possible to be an "I". It's possible to pretend to be an "I," but it's not actually possible to be an "I". That's over.

~

S: When I start watching my breath, it becomes voluntary, meaning I start controlling it. How do I just watch it?

V: In the beginning, discipline's required. In the beginning, when I first started watching my breath, I had to keep bringing my awareness back to the breath through discipline because my mind would start up with its little dreams, with its little thoughts and pull away from the breath, and I had to use discipline to bring awareness back to the breath, so I did. I just used discipline to bring it back. If I caught myself wandering, I'd bring awareness back to the breath and let the mind go which is also another way that I practised surrender or acceptance of life, because I just kept letting the mind go and coming back to the breath. Let the mind go. I loved meditating. I loved that meditation of watching the breath actually, it was really good. It kept me very much in the moment. And after a while, it became easy. But in the beginning, it wasn't easy. In the beginning, it was hard, because I had a habit, like everybody else, of entertaining thoughts, entertaining dreams, so I developed a new practice, the practice of being present to reality which is the practice of meditation. People think, well, I'll meditate 30 minutes a day or an hour a day. We can be in meditation every moment we're awake, if we're present to what's real.

~

S: Does one's guru meet the individual immediately when one dies, and guide them for his or her next birth if one fails to get enlightened, despite all of his practice?

V: I don't think so, but I don't know. You talk about a guru being somewhere in space or here and guiding a person into another life, and that's not my experience. My experience is I have died many times. Hundreds of times. I've gone into the nothingness and then I've been reborn again. On their way into the nothingness, it's very peaceful, and very lovely, and then reborn again as a form, coming back as a fully blown human and doing the whole thing over again.

This lifetime, I started remembering my past lives when I was very young, when I was about 12. I was a Catholic school boy so it was a bit unusual to remember past lives. I just thought I was dreaming, but I was actually remembering my last life and how I died. That was the first memory. And then I started remembering what I did in that life and how I thought in that life and it continued. Some years later, I started remembering lives before that.

We've been here many times, but I don't know if the guru does any guiding. That hasn't been my experience. So I just don't know the answer to that question. I'd have to put it in the "maybe" column because I don't know. One thing I do know is if you do remember all of your past lives, you don't want to come back here and do this again because as human beings we're imprisoned in our minds in a lot of ways. The bars of the mind are made of fear, but we can get out of it. We can wake up to our true nature and be free. And that's what Enlightenment is: freedom. And that is the potential of all human beings to flower and know self as Truth.

Thank you for satsang. Good to see you bravehearts here today.

CHAPTER THIRTEEN

You Have Always Been At Your Final Destination

V: Welcome to satsang.
S: Hello Vishrant. Can you please talk about the topic: you have always been at your final destination?
V: When I was a seeker, I was looking for something. I was looking for Beingness. I was looking for awakening, and as a seeker I was thirsty. I was in desire for Truth. It wasn't until I started experiencing self, true self, that I realised it was always here. It had never been anywhere else. It was always here. It just wasn't aware of itself. So as a seeker, I was aware of my mind and what it thought, and through my senses the world. I was looking for Beingness somehow outside of myself, even though my teachers had said it's within. I was still looking outside thinking that it was somewhere to get, the farther shore, something like that. It wasn't until awareness turned back on itself that the mind realised it's always been here.

I've always been at the final destination, always, and so has everybody else. So this seeking and questing which goes on really needs to turn inward and then such a laugh arises because it's so funny. You've been looking for it for so long in the wrong places and it's always been here. Pure awareness, that that you are, is here, always here, untouchable like the sky, always here. But we get focused on the clouds, the things that appear in the sky, the things that appear in Beingness. We get distracted by watching them and thinking somehow that's going to help us. Really, what's watching? What's aware? It's always here. You're already at your final destination.

Are there any questions, any statements or any challenges to this teaching today?

S: So no matter what I'm doing, does my awareness have to be always looking back for Beingness?

V: If you want Enlightenment, yes. If you want to find yourself as Truth and to exist as that instead of living as the false self, the "I", yes. You have to look back. You have to see what is aware, what is witnessing everything. What is this that's here before the mind begins? Another way of putting it is "Who are you really?"

S: If you want Enlightenment, how do you tangibly know you are successfully turning awareness toward itself?

V: Well, first I found that it was difficult because I wasn't finding anything. It wasn't till I realised that Beingness is not a thing that you can find as such. It's not an object. It's not an experience. In fact, in the early stages of self-inquiry, it was more like nothingness. More like just an emptiness, a silence and a stillness. So, because we're programmed to look for things that move and make noise, we miss it. Our primal programming for survival gets in the way, but it's always here. It's always here. After a while, the silence and stillness felt like it went on forever. There didn't seem to be a boundary of any kind either in depth or width. It was just continuous, infinite, and in looking, in looking at it through the mind, there was an experience of expansion happening in the mind. In continuing to look and continuing to self-inquire, it was a little bit like walking around a big abyss of nothingness and watching it, just walking around it and watching it, and then one day instead of watching it through the mind, it was the knowing of it as self. So there was no watching. It was self now.

It's difficult to describe because we love reference points and in Beingness there are no reference points. It really is the vast emptiness or the vast nothingness of everything and it's very beautiful.

~

S: Is the moment when awareness turns towards itself the same moment the ego dies?

V: So in my experience, I started having satoris. A satori is a glimpse of who we are, and in those satoris, there was no ego, there was just everything as self. Everything as self. It was vast, vast everything as self. There wasn't any ego present. In self-inquiry, turning awareness back to itself, sometimes there was a bit of ego present, and sometimes there wasn't, but when awareness became fully aware of itself ego just disappeared, and from the mind's perspective of understanding, it was clearly seeing that the ego could not possibly have been who I was, not possible because we are Beingness – not because of any intellectual understanding, but because of the direct knowing that occurs when awareness is aware of itself in this moment. So people try for intellectual understanding, they try to understand Enlightenment, they try to understand how to get there, but really, you can't understand it. You can know it and then you're gonna have a lot of trouble explaining it, but you can't understand it. Any conceptual understanding, ideology, belief system is still dreaming. It's still in the mind. The direct knowing is different. It has no reference points. Just is, because you just are. Nothing more, nothing less. You just are.

~

S: If I'm not knowing being as myself, do you think there is any value in understanding that I am Beingness or should I just focus on being present?

V: The thirst for Truth, the thirst to come home to true self is required for the seeker to do whatever is required to come home. In the thirst for higher consciousness, for Truth, a person will meditate, they will self-inquire, they will learn to remove any obstacle that might be in the way of that. To understand that there is something greater than the "I" is important, otherwise why would you look? Why would you be interested? All of the awakened sages supply a light so people can see that there's something else here, that there's different types of people on the planet. There are people who are living ego-based reality and there are people who are actually living Being-based reality, and there is a vast difference. One is false and one is real. The false self, the ego, pretends to be real. But without imagination, it does not exist and imagination is not real. Our true self is always here and it's not imagined. It's always here. So the seeker needs to get an understanding that this is a possibility before they really go for it and have a look outside of the small parameters of what is believed to be real.

~

S: Vishrant, when I'm in my Beingness I can experience an intensity in my throat area and in my belly. Why is this and what can I do about it?

V: Okay. So that has nothing to do with Beingness. That has everything to do with some physiological reaction, energetic or otherwise. I just accept whatever is. You see the questioning at that stage is going to take you back into the mind because the mind is looking to understand, and in a way that is in the way. If we move to acceptance, this is what is, we stop thinking about it, which is brilliant because now we're not engaging the dream machine. Now, awareness can just simply witness itself. Anything that appears can be accepted or we can try to understand it, but understanding is the booby prize. Just accept things as they appear. Be tenderly okay with whatever appears. How's that?

S: Yes. So do we just keep on being in our Beingness when that occurs? Just accept it without putting any sort of thought to it, just remain as Beingness? Is that what you're trying to tell me?

V: Well, you don't have any choice in that because you are Beingness no matter what. It's a matter of where awareness is at – whether awareness is witnessing itself or whether it's actually witnessing the mind, and its story about "Oh, something happening in my throat and my chest". Just keep awareness on itself.

S: Okay. Yeah. Okay.

V: The moment we engage the mind, the chances are awareness is going to go back to the mind, particularly in the early stages of awakening because it has a habit of being locked on the mind. Just witness pure awareness if you can. You can witness experiences happening, that's not a problem, but as far as the mind is concerned accepting them as they are is best rather than trying to understand them.

S: Okay, okay, thank you Vishrant.

~

S: What is the difference between the seer, witness and awareness?

V: None really, unless, of course, it's going through the mind in a way that the mind has actually set itself up as the seer, or the mind has set itself up as awareness or the mind has set itself up as the witness. The mind is a very, very tricky piece of equipment. It can take ownership of just about anything and it tends to. That that's aware of the mind is not an identity. It just is. But the mind can set itself up as an identity and pretend to be awareness because it's that tricky. And it is that good at imagining things. But what's aware of it all? What's aware of the thoughts? Just allow yourself to be the witness of the mind, the witness of everything without thought, without judgment, just the witness. No identity. And see.

~

S: Do some people have bigger and stronger egos than others?

V: Heck, yeah. Some people do weightlifting for their egos. I mean, we look at how the ego develops in a child, how it strengthens itself. It strengthens itself through "no", "no" – resistance. The same as muscles get greater in size through resistance, the ego gets greater in size through resistance. The more resistant a person is, the more likely they've got a big ego, and so in higher consciousness, as you're going for it, instead of becoming bigger, better and more powerful, which is personal growth, you're actually diminishing, you're diminishing ego. It's getting smaller, it's getting left out. So you become less than, rather than more than, but there's definitely a difference in the ego size in people, though it's all simply identification. In other words, pure awareness does not have identification. It just is and it is always here. It doesn't matter how big your ego is or how small your ego is. Just start watching the mind. Just start witnessing it. See what you can see, without judgment. Just watch it, and if you feel to self-inquire, ask the question when a thought arises, "What's aware? What's aware?" Attempt to turn that that is aware of the mind, that is witnessing the mind, back to itself.

~

S: Does being aware of awareness or when awareness is aware of itself, as you put it, suggest three entities, even if two of the three are illusory?

V: There's only one. It's Beingness. There is only one. Everything else is illusionary. There's only one. Awareness turns back on itself and you discover there is only one. There is no such thing as duality. That's a dream. There is only one. We are one. And everything is emptiness. And scientists discovered that years ago with the electron microscope. They discovered at the centre of the atom, in the centre of the electron, just emptiness. Sages have been saying it for 10,000 years because that's their direct knowing. It's true, there's only one.

~

S: If I've always been at my final destination, how do I remove the blockages that stop me from seeing it?
V: Well, the main blockage is dreaming. You're dreaming. Every thought you have is a dream. It's not real. Every thought you have is a dream and because your awareness is on that dream, you think it's real. The dream seems real, but it's not real. No thought is real. It might be a bit of energy, but it's not real. And so the main blockage or the main thing in the way of really both higher consciousness and superconsciousness is dreaming, the constant dreaming, the constant thinking, the constant awareness on the mind, rather than on itself.

In turning awareness back to itself through self-inquiry we start to get glimpses of who we really are and it's not a dream, it is reality. And in this reality, dream appears and disappears like the clouds appear and disappear in the sky. But the interest is in the sky, not the clouds anymore.

When the interest for the mind becomes the sky, then the mind supports self-inquiry, it supports the witness, instead of supporting itself, instead of supporting dreaming. Nothing you think is real. And nothing you think you are is real. Awareness is real, and it's always here. It's always here. Pure awareness, before the mind even begins, it is here. Find that and you've found self. Find that and you're home. You've always been at your final destination, and you finally realised it. It's here now.

~

S: In self-inquiry, I don't notice the thoughts arise, but I am actively thinking every time I drift off from self-inquiry. How can I get to the point where I can notice the thoughts arising before I get caught in thinking?

V: A lot of discipline is required. I stopped teaching pure Advaita Vedanta some 10 years ago because I realised that the methodology that actually works, inquiring into every thought that arises, is only really suitable for people who are in ashrams or monasteries or caves. It's too intense. This is why I started teaching Buddhism because Buddhism is a Way of the Heart. It's also a way of discipline. I feel quite strongly that for those people who are in the marketplace with families and jobs that they can't just inquire into every thought that arises into the mind, "What's aware?" But what they can do is practise openness, and practise being a loving person. In practising openness, we remove all of the obstacles that are in the way of Heart and we remove all the obstacles that are in the way of Enlightenment. Openness counts for everything. This is the Way of the Heart. It's a non-resistant pathway.

Self-inquiry, which is a discipline like meditation, or meditative practices, can also be applied at the same time so you have two wings: one, discipline with self-inquiry, meditations, maybe yoga asanas, and the other one, openness, removing all obstacles and defences that are in the way. Now you have two wings. And with these two wings you can fly and find yourself as Truth. I don't just advise one methodology. The methodology of discipline by itself is probably okay for people who are locking themselves away from the world in some way, but for people in the marketplace, openness counts for everything.

~

S: There are days I feel low in energy and that I think makes it more difficult to say "yes" to situations. What do you think and suggest doing then?

V: I discovered a long, long time ago that we learn surrender through the practise of acceptance. We don't learn surrender through the practise of resistance. And so when obstacles appeared that seemed unreasonable, or that I didn't want to play with, I would practise acceptance. In the practise of acceptance I taught my mind to lie down, and I found Heart, I found love in that openness. So if you're feeling tired, what a great opportunity to practise acceptance. For me, existence gave me chronic fatigue for nearly 15 years, from the age of 34 onwards, and having chronic fatigue and trying to manage your family and your business is difficult because you're tired all of the time. It taught me how to run on empty, doing the most amount with the least amount of effort. I called it "running on empty". It also taught me to accept life as it was rather than how I preferred it to be. In that acceptance, my Heart opened because openness supports love. So don't see tiredness as an obstacle. See it as an opportunity to practise acceptance.

~

S: What practice will you recommend to someone who wants to get on the path and suffers from ADHD?
V: Attention Deficit Hyperactivity Disorder. Well, not many of you would know that I have ADHD. I have had it since I was a child and I was diagnosed with it and it was one of the reasons I got into meditation because it allowed my mind to settle down. My mind doesn't talk to itself anymore so the ADHD doesn't show up very much. But boy, did it cause some problems when I was in school because I wasn't diagnosed until I left school, so I wasn't treated with dexamphetamine or Ritalin or whatever they treat the condition with. So I was just a troublemaker which taught me a lot about acceptance because I was unacceptable at school. I had to learn to find a way to accept myself.

What I did with the ADHD is I went into jobs that demanded a lot of activity all of the time. I was in the band booking business and I used to book heavy metal bands into hotels all around Western Australia and then I went from that into publishing. Now, I don't know if any of you have had anything to do with publishing, but it is full on. I had 30 salesmen working and five clerical staff and dozens of magazines going out each week. There were just so many things to look at and so many things to do. It really served my ADHD mind because I didn't have to concentrate on anything for too long, I had something else to do.

Then I discovered meditation, and in meditation I found that I could find peace from this. I also discovered there were different things I was doing in my life that were allowing me to find peace. One of them was diving underwater. I used to dive with tanks and I used to free dive and I found that every time I got into the water, my mind would slow down and stop. I'd just be with the fish and seaweed and the sand. It was lovely. It was like a reprieve from a noisy mind. I also found that riding motorbikes allowed that too because when you're riding a motorbike, if you're not present, well you're going to die. You have to be present. You can't be lost in your head thinking. So when I started meditating, I realised that these things, diving and motorbikes and martial arts and other things I was into, allowed me to become more present to the moment and took me away from my noisy mind, and I could find the same in meditation.

So meditation for me became something I did every day starting at six in the morning with dynamic meditation, which was a Rajneesh, Osho Rajneesh meditation, and five or six in the evening with kundalini which was another meditation of Rajneesh, Osho Rajneesh. I did these every day for years and years and years. I just loved meditating. I got to the stage where I was just sitting and watching my breath because it was so profoundly peaceful.

So you can do it, but you have to really want to. You have to really want to because if we want something badly enough we'll do whatever it takes to make it so. I loved meditation so much that I discovered I wanted to be in meditation all of the time. Present to reality all of the time. I had lost interest in dreaming and I still have lost interest in dreaming. This moment is so precious. I hope that helps.

~

S: I thought I was living in the moment until I met people who were more present than me. How would I know if I'm present enough for waking up?

V: Self-inquiry. That methodology demands that you turn awareness back to itself. "What's aware? What's aware of the mind? What's aware?" You're coming into the moment because you're becoming aware of what's real. In walking, you be aware of your footfalls, you be aware of your breath, your arm movements, the sights around you, the sounds around you. If you're aware of all of those things, you'll be in meditation because you won't be able to think, you'll just be able to be with what is. So we can practise meditation all day long if we want by simply being aware of what is happening around us, our feelings in our hands, our feelings in our feet, the sounds around us, the sights around us. It's up to you. We were pretty much like that to some degree before we went to school and then we went to school and we learnt to live in our heads. Most human adults live in their heads until they die, thinking that somehow they're living, but they're really just existing in a dream.

Reclaim reality from the dream that you got lost in by going to school. Reclaim it with the practise of meditation. It works.

~

S: From experience of satoris that I've had, I understand that there is only now. Yet I still get caught in fear and hope. What would give me a deeper understanding that there is only now?

V: The deeper understanding wouldn't help you one bit because you already understand it. You understand that there is only now, you already understand that, but you have a habit of dreaming. Fear and hope belong to projections of the future, not real, but you have a habit of projecting. You have to change the pattern. I love the now and I love the unknown, so I practised being present to reality until that became my pattern. Whatever we practise becomes our pattern. If you've practised being present to reality long enough, you'll find yourself present to reality. If all you practise is thinking, well, that's all you're ever going to be good at: thinking – and thinking is not real.

~

S: Is it possible to speak more about openness? How does this translate in relationships?

V: Yeah. Without openness – we'll go on the negative first – without openness, there is no love. There might be the pretence of love, there might be the thinking there's love, but if we're closed, we can't even perceive love. Love is perceived in openness, not in closure. And when there is love, there is intimacy.

And intimacy also is perceived in openness, not in closure. If we're closed, we might believe that we're loving, we might believe we're experiencing love, but that's highly unlikely because we've cut ourselves off, we've created a barrier. In openness, we as an "I" start disappearing, and because we start disappearing, the main obstacle in the way of the perception of love is disappearing. So if you want to be really loving, get out of the way. Leave yourself at the door. Sometimes you go into these Buddhist temples and above the door, it says "abandon all hope". Hope belongs to the mind. Just leave it behind. Leave all of the thoughts behind. Be present to reality. It's lovely. Openness is the most wonderful thing we human beings can get involved with. But we don't live in a world that is open. We live in a world that is basically closed. People are defended because they're frightened of being hurt and they've developed patterns of closure. You want to fully live? Open up. Wear your Heart on your sleeve and walk through the world vulnerable. This is the Beauty Way. This is the Way of the Heart.

~

S: When I'm in low energy, I get angry more easily and sometimes hurt the ones I love, and that worries me. I don't want that to happen, but my feelings take me over. Can you please comment?

V: Yeah, you've become a victim of your own feelings. That's not a good idea. When you say your feelings take you over, you've become a victim of them. Your feelings don't take you over at all. You're reacting. You, you're reacting, because you're tired. And my suggestion is simple: instead of reacting, accept life as it is, accept the problems that present themselves when you're tired as they are instead of reacting. That would mean you taking full responsibility for yourself, that you make yourself feel, not the world around you. That is the ultimate in maturity. I make myself feel no matter what anyone else does or says, at any time, whether I'm tired or not tired. I make myself feel, therefore I'm fully responsible for my reactions. It's up to you. Have a look and see who makes you feel.

~

S: Can I say that love is not a feeling, but the presence in the Heart that is open and infinite?
V: It's so funny because I can't find a location for love. It's everywhere. Some people say it's in the chest. I just . . . it's everywhere. "Love is in the air, everywhere you look around." I can't say that it's anywhere. But when there is an absence of the "I", when there's an absence of you, love is easy to perceive. When there's a lot of you in the picture, a defensive survival mechanism, an "I", there's usually a sense of separation and a lack of the sense of love.

So in learning to get out of the picture, in learning to get out of the way, you will find more love, but as far as it being in the Heart, I don't know. I just find it everywhere. When I'm inside, there's nothing, just nothing. When I'm out here with people, there's love. It's a mystery to me, but I know one thing: openness counts for everything.

~

S: How do I explain to another person that they are dreaming?

V: I don't. I just talk to seekers and I tell them they're dreaming if they're dreaming. I don't tell the people out there in the marketplace they're dreaming. It wouldn't be accepted. "Look you, stop dreaming, you wake up to your true nature." You can't tell that many people about it. Most people can't understand. They have no concept of what you're talking about. None. They believe themselves to be real. They believe they are a mind and they are a body that's been somewhere and is going somewhere. So why would you want to bother trying to convince them of anything else? I'm here for seekers who want to know the Truth and they've got to come to me. I'm not a missionary. I'm not trying to save the world. If people are interested in knowing the Truth, they can come and say hello. But I'm not going to try and convince anyone of anything. That would be me being crazy. I just point. I point in a certain direction. You have a look. You look and see for yourself.

~

S: I find much happiness when holding my baby, but when I switch into business mode, I feel myself harder, not ready for what's coming. How to switch between the two and not close?

V: So when you're holding your baby, you're holding something that is harmless and defenceless, and so there's no threat to you whatsoever, you can be wide open. It's easy to be wide open with babies and puppies. The trick for us human beings is: can we be wide open with people who are dangerous, people who might hurt us? Can we be wide open in business and still operate? My experience is yes we can, but it takes a lot of practice because we're very practised at being defended. We're very practised at being closed, protecting ourselves, and that's our, usually, our default patterning. To undo that, we have to practise the opposite. We have to practise being open. Now we know we can be open with babies and probably puppies. If we can be open with puppies and babies, we can be open with everyone. It's just a matter of choice. Choose openness. Choose to be vulnerable. Drop your defence systems. Love the world.

~

S: So can I say peace, love and joy are the jewels of consciousness?
V: The only jewel of consciousness is love because love is real. Peace is related to the mind. The mind is not real. Love is real. So the true jewel of consciousness is love. What the mind thinks about that is also not real. Whether it finds peace or not, that's not real either. What's real, though, is love. The mind is imagined. Love is not imagined. It is real and it is here. If you're open enough, you can perceive it. If you are not open, you may not. It's your choice because it is your responsibility for your openness.

~

S: How can I juggle the chaos of running a busy business, but still be open and in touch with Beingness?
V: It can be difficult. I don't even know if that's possible. I don't know.

Awakening occurs. And then the person who awakens can either be in the world or not in the world. If they choose to be in the world, it's going to be harder for them because there's going to be so many things that are going to try to pull awareness away from itself, back to the mind, back to the ego. But with practice – the practice of letting go from the mind's perspective – awareness seems to stay quite solidly on itself, a bit like two permanent magnets stuck on like that. That tends to happen a bit down the track, not straightaway. Someone who's just waking up will find it fragile. Awareness flip flops, from the mind back to itself, and if the mind is constantly contracting, well, awareness gets locked on the mind.

The mind can support awakening, support Enlightenment, by not contracting, by not resisting life, by accepting life as it is whether you're in business or you're not in business, whether it's hectic or not. Can you be in a state of acceptance? Or are you going to go to a state of resistance? In resistance, in contraction, awareness gets attracted to that. So a mind that supports Enlightenment is a mind that is equanimous. It's a mind that stays even no matter what is happening.

~

S: Does it matter whether one stays in the world or not after awakening?

V: No, it doesn't matter. But my teacher and spiritual master Osho Rajneesh said if you find the light, don't hide it, don't hide it away, don't lock it away. Take it into the marketplace and shine it so others may see. So here we are. But it doesn't matter really. As a matter of fact, nothing matters. It's a love affair. The mind has a love affair with Truth, the beloved, and in that love affair with Truth the mind becomes a servant of Truth. The mind becomes a servant of love and as a servant of love and as a servant of Truth, the mind becomes a servant of humanity because we are one.

~

S: Is it enough to rest as awareness and stop going along with or being drawn to thoughts on a continuous basis? Will that one practice eventually end contraction?

V: The only thing that ends contraction is acceptance of life as it is and that becomes a practice. We're all programmed to resist life as it is. That's our primal programming for survival. So for that to change, we have to practise something different. My understanding is that the practise of acceptance of life as it is teaches us surrender, which is actually a non-doing. I don't know of any other way that really works. Acceptance works.

So we can go a bit further and we can start talking about, well, what creates contraction? And we can look in the mind and see, well, it's usually when an expectation isn't met somewhere. We have a belief system on how things should be and we have an expectation based on that belief system. When the expectation's not met, we contract because we think something's wrong. We can undo the belief system, which disempowers it the moment we put doubt into it, and we can accept that this is how it is rather than right or wrong, good or bad. This is simply what is. It is neither right nor wrong, good nor bad. It is simply what is. With this understanding and this practice, the mind can stay level. Up to you. Whatever you practise, you're going to be good at. If all you do is practise resistance to life, that's all you'll ever be good at.

~

S: Is Beingness in everything like plants and in water?

V: Okay, so Beingness is everything, yes. There is nothing that isn't Beingness. Everything is Beingness. You can take that on intellectually as an understanding or you can know that directly by turning awareness onto awareness. Then it's not borrowed knowledge, it's your direct knowing of this.

~

S: Are there certain lifestyles, like being in the constant stress of business, that impact being in touch with the final destination?

V: Yeah, some businesses really aren't suited for people who are interested in finding themselves as Truth, it's true, and some businesses are. I was a publisher for 10 years before I gave that up and I gave that up to find my Heart because as a publisher, I found that I was too warlike. Business made me too warlike. I'd been programmed to win and I found that the freneticism of business was too much, so I gave up my businesses so I could find Heart because I recognised that love, which is Heart, is the true jewel of consciousness. At that time in my life, when I was 33, 34, I recognised I was pretty broke. I had been successful in business, but I was broke because I didn't have Heart, so I went in the pursuit of Heart, and in that pursuit of Heart I gave my businesses to my staff.

I discovered that I had to undo myself as an "I", as a mind. So then the "great undoing" really, really commenced – undoing all of the belief systems that were in the way that kept contracting me, removing all of the defence systems that were in the way, because it was obvious they were in the way – until there was nothing left. It was a bit like reverse engineering. I'd been built as a war machine and I had to reverse engineer that, and I did. It took years, but I did, and I started finding Heart. I started finding the beauty of love, started finding the true jewel of consciousness. In that, I discovered that I still had to be here in the world. I still had to do something, and so what to do if I'm going to be here in the world?

I figured out that to follow love I needed to follow how it affected my mind. Love was affecting my mind by making it feel like taking care of people, taking care of the planet, taking care of plants, taking care of animals – just taking care, generally speaking. So I went back to school and trained as a naturopath and as a psychotherapist so I could have some tools to help people with. My love affair with love dictated that I moved into service of others so I could help, and that love affair is still here today 33 years later. I recommend it to everybody, but it is true that some businesses don't suit the Way of the Heart or

Enlightenment, but you'll have to look for yourself and see if that's true. You have to be terribly honest with yourself, ruthlessly honest with yourself. For me, it was a very expensive thing to do to give away my companies, but it was worth it because love is everything.

Thank you for satsang. Good to see you bravehearts here today.

About Vishrant

Vishrant is a contemporary mystic who offers a pragmatic path to higher consciousness.

He made a fortune in publishing as a young man, retiring at the age of 28, and then as a world traveller and student of personal development later met controversial Indian guru and spiritual teacher Bhagwan "Osho" Shree Rajneesh who initiated him into the world of higher consciousness and enlightenment.

That encounter led to Vishrant tasting unconditional love during a terrifying shipwreck off the Western Australian coast and then glimpsing his own true nature. After these revelations, he gave his multi-million dollar company to the staff who had served him so diligently for a decade, and then set off around Australia barefoot for the next four years while searching for how to open his Heart once and forever.

After Osho's death in 1999, Vishrant committed himself to the Way of the Heart while working as a naturopath and psychotherapist, running men's encounter groups and later serving a crop of Advaita Vedanta teachers who started visiting Western Australia at the end of the 1990s. Vishrant woke up in 1999 in the presence of one of those teachers.

Since then, Vishrant has held satsang and retreats, and runs a Mystery School in the Perth hills which is also available online for those seeking to find their true nature.

Vishrant's teachings are pragmatic and free of belief systems and religious ideologies. He sees himself as a reality teacher rather than a spiritual teacher and says spirituality has become an overused word. His invitation is for people to investigate the Truth through their own direct experience.

To get involved, visit vishrant.org.

www.ingramcontent.com/pod-product-compliance
Lightning Source LLC
Chambersburg PA
CBHW030227100526
44585CB00012BA/280